Advance praise for The Green Psalter:

"Building on the latest work in Psalms study, *The Green Psalter* is not a casual pitch for greater care of our world. Arthur Walker-Jones offers a deep reflection on the Psalms, one that compels the reader to see the creation as God's handiwork and justice as our way in it. Not least among the surprises to be found here are the author's argument that the theme of God as divine warrior is central to the laments and his illuminating discussion of God's deliverance from oppression and death."

Patrick D. Miller

Professor of Old Testament Theology Emeritus
Princeton Theological Seminary

"Is a green reading of the Psalms possible? After all, Psalm 8 declares that humans are a little lower than God but other living creatures are much lower—beneath human feet! Yet Arthur Walker-Jones claims there are spiritual resources in the Psalms that can transform our unhealthy relationship with Earth. Quite a claim! Using a form of canonical criticism, the author recognizes metaphors, such as 'the green tree' in Psalm 1, as powerful clues that just humans identify with Earth rather than rule over it. Within each Psalm genre, metaphors are found that are more than metaphors—they are multivalent messages that God and the righteous are not detached from nature but immersed in nature, intent on liberating rather than dominating creation. This volume is a significant step in the challenge to pursue a serious green reading of the Bible."

Norman Habel

Professorial Fellow
Flinders University, South Australia

— The Green Psalter —

Resources for an
Ecological Spirituality

ARTHUR WALKER-JONES

For Elise

Fortress Press

Minneapolis

THE GREEN PSALTER
Resources for an Ecological Spirituality

Cover Image: "Tree in the Desert," © Claudia Dewald/iStockphoto
Cover design: Laurie Ingram
Book design: PerfecType, Nashville, Tenn.

Library of Congress Cataloging-in-Publication Data
Walker-Jones, Arthur.
  The Green Psalter : resources for an ecological spirituality / Arthur Walker-Jones.
     p. cm.
  Includes bibliographical references and index.
  ISBN 978-0-8006-6302-5 (alk. paper)
  1. Bible. O.T. Psalms—Criticism, interpretation, etc. 2. Ecotheology. I. Title.
BS1430.52.W33 2009
  261.8'8—dc22
                              2008043287

The paper used in this publication meets the minimum requirements of American National Standard for Information Sciences—Permanence of Paper for Printed Library Materials, ANSI Z329.48-1984.

Manufactured in the U.S.A.

12 11 10 09 1 2 3 4 5 6 7 8 9 10

CONTENTS

INTRODUCTION

More science and more technology are not going to get us out
of the present ecological crisis until we find a new religion, or
rethink our old one.

Lynn White Jr.[1]

For years prior to Hurricane Katrina, scientists had been warning
that New Orleans was sinking and that canals and commercial
development were causing the disappearance of the wetlands and
barrier islands that formed natural defenses against storm surges.
On August 29, 2005, Katrina came ashore in southeast Louisiana,
Alabama, and Mississippi. Earlier, Katrina had crossed Florida as a
category-one hurricane, but had increased to a category-five hurricane and picked up rain over the warm waters of the Gulf of Mexico.
When it came ashore in Louisiana, it had decreased to a category-
three hurricane, but the combination of the storm surge and unusu-
ally heavy rains caused several levees to fail in New Orleans, flooding

80 percent of the city. Over eighteen hundred people died in the southern United States, fifteen hundred in Louisiana. For some, Hurricane Katrina was just another natural disaster caused by poorly designed and maintained levees. But, for a growing number of people in the United States and around the world, Katrina was a warning of the dangers of climate change and environmental destruction. Climate change models predict more frequent and violent storms like Katrina.

In the documentary *An Inconvenient Truth*, Al Gore describes global warming as a *moral* issue.[2] He discusses the denial, despair, and myths that keep people from taking action. Several years ago, the Union of Concerned Scientist released a video that made a direct appeal to people of faith for help.[3] Science, they said, had identified the problems, but science alone could not respond to the environmental crisis because the issue was a moral and behavioral one. They appealed to communities of faith for help in changing values and behavior. To that end, this book attempts to retrieve spiritual resources from the Book of Psalms for the transformation of our relationship to Earth.

Why the book of Psalms? Psalms have been read and chanted every week in synagogue and church services for centuries. They provide much of the language and imagery of the Jewish and Christian prayer books, liturgies, hymns, and prayers. As Brevard Childs says, "In the prayer book, the midrashim, and the rituals of the synagogue the all-encompassing presence of the Hebrew Psalter is visible. Similarly for the Christian church, the New Testament is saturated with citations from the Psalter," and "even today many of the most enduring hymns of the church are based on Old Testament psalms."[4] Moreover, both Jews and Christians base their faith on the Bible, and, of all biblical books, the Psalter has the most extensive speech to God and about God. The book of Psalms, therefore, is a good place to begin the retrieval of spiritual resources for a response to the global environmental crisis.

Christianity and Ecology

The problem that needs to be addressed first, however, is that the dominant forms of western Christianity have been at least partially responsible for the environmental crisis. Many environmentalists, therefore, are suspicious of Christianity and either espouse no religion or choose what they feel to be a more ecological religion. I specified *dominant forms of western Christianity* because there are minority traditions, within western Christianity and nonwestern forms of Christianity, that have been more ecological. But these have not been the most influential voices in western culture. I specified *partial responsibility* because there are many contributing factors, but the environmental crisis developed in a supposedly Christian culture, and most churches have been slow to respond. This book makes the case that the Bible has spiritual and ethical resources to address the environmental crisis, but, first, it is important to come to terms with the nature of the criticisms. In my opinion, responses that become defensive before they fully understand the criticisms tend to be shallow and inadequate. It is necessary to understand the criticisms of Christianity before we can begin to identify what might, or might not, be useful ethical and spiritual resources.

Lynn White Jr.'s article, "The Historical Roots of Our Ecological Crisis," first published in 1967, is often cited as a classic criticism of Christianity and clearly and eloquently identifies the issues. Before turning to his criticisms, it should perhaps be noted that White also held out hope for Christianity. He, like the Union of Concerned Scientists, thought science and technology alone were insufficient to address the problem. Since the values that have created the problem derive from Christianity, and those values continue to be widespread in our society even among those who no longer consider themselves Christians, "more science and more technology are not going to get us out of the present ecological crisis until we find a new religion, or rethink our old one."[5] He considers a rethinking of Christianity more viable in our culture and suggests that a direction may be suggested by the spirituality of St. Francis of Assisi,[6] which is deeply indebted to the Psalms.

In his criticism of western Christianity, White argues that, in its interpretation of Genesis 1–3, "No item in the physical creation had any purpose save to serve man's[7] purposes. And, although man's body is made of clay, he is not simply part of nature: he is made in God's image."[8] Thus Christianity considered humanity separate from and superior to nature. "Especially in its Western form," he says, "Christianity is the most anthropocentric religion the world has seen . . . in absolute contrast to ancient paganism and Asia's religions (except, perhaps, Zoroastrianism), [it] not only established a dualism of man and nature but also insisted that it is God's will that man exploit nature for his proper ends."[9] On a popular level, many Christians think Christianity is about saving humans, and they have little interest in Earth because they are going to heaven. Or, in the secular version of this myth, we will travel to other planets, presumably to destroy them, too. In discussions of environmental ethics, Earth has no intrinsic value. It is only valuable in so far as it is useful to humans who are viewed as separate from and superior to nature.

In order to facilitate exploitation, Christianity removed spirit from nature.

> In Antiquity, every tree, every spring, every stream, every hill had its own *genius loci*, its guardian spirit. . . . Before one cut a tree, mined a mountain, or dammed a brook, it was important to placate the spirit in charge of that particular situation, and

to keep it placated. By destroying pagan animism, Christianity made it possible to exploit nature in a mood of indifference to the feelings of natural objects.[10]

In summary, the issues that White identified, and have frequently been repeated in subsequent discussions, are anthropocentrism and dualistic thinking that separates humanity and spirit from nature, thus devaluing it.

Dualisms and Ecojustice

The older tradition of naming hurricanes like Katrina with women's names is one small example of the many ways western culture identifies women with nature. Many feminists have recognized the parallels in theory and practice between the exploitation of nature and women. These ecofeminists recognize the duality between humanity and nature as just one of a number of dualisms in western thought that legitimate oppression. In her book, *Feminism and the Mastery of Nature*, Val Plumwood identifies a number of dualisms, such as:[11]

culture	/	nature
male	/	female
mind, spirit	/	body (nature)
reason	/	emotion
human	/	nature
civilized	/	primitive
subject	/	object

In relation to ecological exploitation, I would add:

spiritual	/	material
heaven	/	earth
animate	/	inanimate

Dualistic or binary thinking legitimates exploitation in western culture because the items in the left-hand column are associated together and considered superior to those in the right-hand column. In order to relate this to other forms of oppression, I would note that western culture's language, images, and stories, often associate white men with the left-hand column and associate women, gays and lesbians, people of color, and indigenous peoples with the right-hand column.

Action on climate change has been hindered by the perception that human suffering and injustice are more important issues than the environment, so it is important to note that social and ecological justice are interrelated. I will use the word *ecojustice* to indicate this interrelationship and interdependence. The use of this term could lead to a couple of misinterpretations. First, when two fields are joined in this way in the sciences, the prefixed one is often of secondary status and importance.[12] In the same way, some uses of *ecojustice* represent a treatment of ecology as an addition to other, more important, issues of justice and do not address the anthropocentrism of the tradition.[13] Second, *ecojustice* may suggest an understanding of ecological justice separate from social justice. For lack of a better term, however, I use *ecojustice* to indicate the interrelationship and interdependence of issues of ecological and social justice.

Ecofeminism and the dualisms outlined above point to the interrelationship of ecological and social justice. In the aftermath of Hurricane Katrina, the interdependence of issues of poverty, race, and ecology were in full view. It was the poor, mostly African American population, of New Orleans who had to take buses or stay in their homes, and who were left in the Superdome. After the waters receded, it was easier for the wealthy to return and find work than for the poor. As a result, the percentage of the population who are African American has declined significantly. For this reason, this book will draw attention to the interrelationship of social and ecological justice in the Psalter.

Green Biblical Interpretation

Early treatments of biblical interpretation and the environment tended to be apologetic and superficial, often focusing on the interpretation of "dominion" in Gen 1:26-27. The typical argument was that, although "dominion" is royal language, the image of the ideal king in the ancient Near East, and other biblical texts like Psalm 72, was one who cared for the poor and the oppressed. Humans created in the image of God would care for creation as stewards of a just king. The royal language, however, remains troubling. Some note that in Ps 72:8, the enemies of the king are forced to lick the dust.[14] In addition, the image of humans as "stewards" maintains humans as separate from and above nature.

The problem, however, is much deeper than the interpretation of a particular text. There are passages throughout the Bible that could either support anthropocentrism and dualism or could support ecocentrism and the interdependence of all creation. Often much depends on the reader and his or her method of interpretation. Therefore, an examination of other parts of the Bible and the development of ecological principles of interpretation are necessary.

The first sustained criticism of the Bible from the perspective of Earth is contained in the Earth Bible Series, five volumes published from 2000 to 2002 by an international group of biblical scholars. The Earth Bible series borrowed a method of suspicion and retrieval from feminist hermeneutics of the Bible. The contributors would first approach texts with the suspicion that they legitimated environmental exploitation. Only then would they turn to materials that might be retrieved for an ecological interpretation. The theologians and biblical scholars who initiated this series developed six ecojustice principles in conversation with ecologists to guide the writers of individual articles. They are:

1. *The Principle of Intrinsic Worth.* The universe, Earth, and all its components have intrinsic worth/value.
2. *The Principle of Interconnectedness.* Earth is a community of interconnected living things that are mutually dependent on each other for life and survival.
3. *The Principle of Voice.* Earth is a subject capable of raising its voice in celebration and against injustice.
4. *The Principle of Purpose.* The universe, Earth, and all its components are part of a dynamic cosmic design within which each piece has a place in the overall goal of that design.
5. *The Principle of Mutual Custodianship.* Earth is a balanced and diverse domain where responsible custodians can function as partners, rather than rulers, to sustain a balanced and diverse Earth community.
6. *The Principle of Resistance.* Earth and its components not only suffer from injustices at the hands of humans, but actively resist them in the struggle for justice.[15]

I wrote a chapter on Psalm 104 in the Earth Bible,[16] and my involvement in the project was important in developing my thinking about ecological interpretation of the Bible. The usefulness of principles four and five have been questioned by some and have been less important for my work. The scientific basis of a cosmic design with a purpose is questionable, and the past use of "progress" to legitimate exploitation of Earth makes some environmentalists suspicious of principle four. For some, principle five, custodianship, is too close to stewardship, which is problematic because it maintains the separation between humanity and nature.

The other principles have been more important to my work because they help to identify and overcome anthropocentrism and the dualisms that have legitimated ecological destruction. The first principle, intrinsic worth, helps counteract the effects of dualisms between subject and object, animate and inanimate, humanity and nature, that legitimate the view in western culture that everything has value only as it is useful to human beings. The second principle, interconnectedness, is fundamental to ecological science, helps to overcome the dualism between humanity and nature, and recognizes humans as interconnected and interdependent with all other parts of Earth community. Principle three, voice, and principle six, resistance, seek to treat the Earth as a subject, rather than as an object. Thus the writers in the series sought to avoid using the definite article with Earth and speak of "Earth" instead of "the earth." Therefore, this work uses the Earth Bible's ecojustice principles, especially the intrinsic worth, voice, and resistance of Earth, to help identify and overcome the dualisms that have legitimated exploitation.

Metaphors and Society

As someone concerned with the future of the planet and an occasional activist, I want to understand the role of the Bible in either obstructing or facilitating social change. I would like to provide resources for changing attitudes, behavior, and political will. For more than a century, however, biblical scholarship has focused on what the Bible meant in ancient Israel and, as a result, has had difficulty talking about what the Bible means today or, perhaps more importantly, its contemporary social function. Historical criticism has been, and largely continues to be, the dominant methodology in biblical scholarship. Even newer methods are often absorbed into the historical paradigm by being confined to investigations of what the Bible meant to ancient readers and writers.

An interesting feature of the current theological landscape is that whereas historical criticism used to be perceived as the preserve of liberals, now it is being embraced by conservatives. Both liberal and conservative uses of historical criticism, however, seem to be based on faulty assumptions. Liberal Christians often use historical criticism to relativize the authority of the Bible. They point to the existence of diverse positions in the Bible or argue that statements come from a far different cultural context than ours. Yet they are bewildered by their inability to educate a broader public in this historical perspective and by the continuing influence of the Bible in society. Conservatives seem to assume that a study of grammar and historical context, even if it is complicated by criticism, will determine the meaning of a text and provide an authoritative foundation for theology and ethics. This ideal is undermined by the multitude of interpretations within conservative churches. Moreover, most contemporary philosophical and literary theories of meaning hold that texts have multiple meanings and that reading communities play a significant role in constructing meaning, not to mention social function. Both liberal and conservative uses of historical criticism have tended to make conceptual, theological bridges between ancient text and contemporary society that fail to understand the social power of the Bible.

In my understanding, metaphors and narratives have greater social and political power than concepts. For instance, leading feminist theologian Sallie McFague notes that the image of God as male has far more social influence than any doctrine of the transcendence of God.[17] Thus, feminist theologians are suspicious of male metaphors for God and seek to retrieve female or androgynous ones. In a series of books, McFague has worked with a number of metaphors including the image of Earth as the body of God as the basis for an ecotheology.[18] In addition to the Earth Bible principles, an ecological interpretation needs a methodology that can comprehend and analyze the contemporary social power of biblical symbols.

Northrop Frye

Several insights from the work of Northrop Frye are useful for understanding the contemporary social power of biblical imagery and stories. Frye was an internationally renowned literary critic, probably the leading North American literary critic of his day, and a United Church of Canada minister. His *Anatomy of Criticism*, an introduction to literary critical method, remains a classic.[19] He also wrote several books on the Bible and literature.[20] Ironically, his work is seldom referred to or used by biblical scholars.[21] In the previous generation, his literary perspectives on the Bible were alien and challenging to the historical criticism that dominated biblical scholarship. Now that newer literary critical methods are more common in biblical scholarship, other literary critics are in vogue. Some of Frye's insights, however, are still valuable for biblical interpretation. Frye's methodology provides insights for interpreting the Psalms in three areas.

First, Frye understands literature as symbolic meditations on the future of society. According to Fredric Jameson, "The greatness of Frye, and the radical difference between his work and that of the great bulk of garden-variety myth criticism, lies in his willingness to raise the issue of community and draw basic, essentially social interpretive consequences from the nature of religion as collective representation." With Frye, he would see all literature "as a weaker form of myth" and concludes that "all literature, no matter how weakly, must be informed by what we have called a political unconscious, that literature must be read as a symbolic meditation on the destiny of community."[22] This book will analyze the psalms as social, symbolic meditations on reality and the future of society—especially humanity's relation to nature.

Second, Frye's work makes a lasting contribution to myth criticism. In a recent book on myth criticism as a literary-critical method, Laurence Coupe treats Frye's understanding of myth as one of the most sophisticated.[23]

The use of the word "myth" in relation to the Bible is immediately at risk of creating misunderstanding among Christians and Jews. In English, a frequent meaning of myth is something fictitious and untrue. Fiction, however, is not necessarily untrue. As Frye and Jameson suggest, fiction reflects on the future of society, imagines what reality we may create. It expresses deeply held values that shape our behavior and create reality. Frye points out that, in a rapidly changing world, fiction may have as much access to truth and reality as science and history. Science fiction, far from being untrue or unreal, may very quickly become scientific and historical reality.

It is important to bear in mind, that central to Frye's method is an expanded understanding of what Aristotle terms *mythos*. For Frye, *mythos* is a narrative pattern with associated images that appear repeatedly in literature. Thus, when we are reading a book or watching a movie from one of our favorite genres, we recognize typical characters and may guess where the story is going because certain characters and story lines are typical of that genre. In my thinking, this is a contributing factor to the social power of some metaphors and images.[24] Certain types of stories are told repeatedly in a society because they are part of that society's understanding of reality, their worldview. Many readers will associate these images with the narratives that construct their reality. For instance, some have criticized George Bush's foreign policy by saying he was acting like a cowboy. In the western movie genre, conflicts almost inevitably need to be resolved by force. Evidently, the critics of Bush thought the western as a genre was informing personal behavior and public policy. The *mythos* of a film genre was creating an *ethos*. Although the cowboy image was used negatively by Bush's critics, it undoubtedly has positive connotations that are important for U.S. identity and values. Fiction, far from being untrue, is a guide for behavior, creating reality and shaping the future. For Frye, *mythoi* are recurring cultural narratives and images that different interests in society use to imagine the future.

Third, Frye's understanding of *mythos* is related to another area in which his work continues to be important for literary critics, that is, in the study of genre. As the example above of the western already suggests, a genre tends to have typical narrative patterns, characters, and images. In my interpretation, identifying these narrative structures and images provides a way of connecting the Bible to contemporary culture. I identify recurring patterns in the Bible, compare them to similar narratives and imagery in contemporary culture, and reflect on the way they understand reality and envision the future. In summary, certain *mythoi* are characteristic of certain genres and can be analyzed as social, symbolic reflections on reality.

Northrop Frye's method provides me with a way of connecting genre criticism to contemporary cultural criticism that helps to analyze the ecological potential of images. Some may notice in the examples I use that, in contrast to Frye who uses examples from the "canon" of western literature, my examples and thus my definitions of literature and culture tend to be more popular. The patterns in popular culture provide simpler and clearer illustrations and have a more direct and widespread influence on society. Books and movies are the stories contemporary society tells about the nature of reality.

The following section relates these insights to current, scholarly methods of interpreting the book of Psalms.

Reading the Psalms

Even when historical criticism was the only method in biblical studies, it was not very useful in Psalms studies. The general lack of historical references in most psalms made it difficult to date them. Psalms used a lot of stereotypical language and showed signs of being developed and used over centuries. Instead, the dominant method among Psalms scholars of the previous generation became genre or form criticism. It remains influential with the current generation. In biblical studies, genre criticism categorizes psalms into types and analyzes them based on their form and content. It also speculates about the setting-in-life (*Sitz im Leben*) or typical social or religious situation in which a genre would have been used. The major genres that biblical scholars identify in the Psalms are lament, thanksgiving, and hymns.[25] There are a number of other subgenres, less frequently occurring genres, and mixtures. Scholars debate the names, form, content, and setting-in-life of the genres, but in general agree on the existence of the genres and the usefulness of the method. In literary criticism, the study of genres has developed since being adopted in biblical studies, and literary critics now use more than form and content in the analysis of genres. This book furthers genre research in the Psalter by adding narrative patterns, characters, and images to the analysis of the genres. These are then related to contemporary narratives and ecological interpretation.

Some might object that the method I am proposing ignores unique historical and literary features by focusing on what is typical. This is the criticism of genre criticism that was made by James Muilenburg, the founder of what came to be known in Hebrew Bible studies as rhetorical criticism.[26] I would argue that knowledge of the typical is necessary in order to appreciate what is unique and vice versa. While the broad scope of this study means that I will not be able to do justice either to the description of what is typical or attend to all the unique features, I do hope to make some progress along that path. I will discuss the way both typical and unique features contribute to the meaning of the Psalter.

Whereas genre criticism was the most commonly used method of the previous generation of biblical scholars, much recent Psalms scholarship uses canonical criticism. It was first developed by Brevard Childs as a way to overcome the shortcomings of historical interpretation.[27] He said that genre criticism created a rupture with the traditional interpretation of the Psalter in church and synagogue. Genre criticism focused on the psalms as ancient prayers to God, but church and synagogue had interpreted the Psalter as scripture, or God's words to humanity.[28] Canonical criticism studies the way individual psalms were organized into a book as indications of the way the compilers intended them to be interpreted theologically.[29] More of the evidence for this finding will be discussed in the next chapter, but, by way of anticipation, canonical criticism has discovered that the Psalter was edited to be read as scripture. While I do not think the intentions of the editors can determine contemporary meaning and social function, canonical critics have provided a great service by highlighting features of the Psalter that allow contemporary readers to find meaning in it as a book or as scripture.

Subsequent chapters will provide more detailed evidence of the editing of the Psalter, but, by way of anticipation, the main points can be briefly summarized here. Doxologies separate the Psalter into five books. From an early period, the five books of the Psalter were understood to be analogous to the Torah. Just as the first five books of the Bible were the teachings of Moses, the five books of the Psalter were the teachings of David. This work furthers the discussion of the canonical shape of the Psalter by showing how the narrative patterns of the genres also shape the story of the entire collection.

In this task I am particularly indebted to Nancy L. deClaissé-Walford for her work in weaving together the insights of other scholars to show how the Psalter can be read as a "story of identity and existence for the postexilic community."[30] She shows clearly how the various books of the Psalter correspond to various periods in Israel's history and that the Psalter "was read publicly to remind the Israelites of their story—the majestic reign of King David, the dark days of oppression and exile, the restoration of the glorious reign of Yahweh, and the surety that Israel could continue to exist as a 'nation' in the ancient Near East."[31] This book will show the contribution made to the story of the Psalter by recurring narrative patterns and images in the major genres.

In recent biblical scholarship there has been much interest in the role of symbols and metaphors.[32] William Brown's book, *Seeing the Psalms*, made a significant contribution to our understanding of the role of imagery in the poetry of the Psalms.[33] *The Green Psalter* furthers that discussion by attempting to understand the power of certain images and analyze their relation to the *ethos* of society.

As concern for environmental issues has grown in society, so has interest in biblical theologies of creation. A debate has arisen about whether creation is repressive or liberative. In a conversation between Richard Middleton and Walter Brueggemann in the *Harvard Theological Review*, Middleton questioned Brueggemann's treatment of creation as legitimating the status quo because his experience as a Trinidadian was that creation was liberating and he found support for that view in the Hebrew Bible.[34] Similarly, writers in the Earth Bible Series question the assumption that creation theology is necessarily good for Earth community.[35] This book shows that creation theologies play an important role in the story of the Psalter and can be interpreted in ways that are liberating for Earth community.

The following chapters are organized both according to genre and according to the canonical shape of the Psalter. Chapter 1 discusses wisdom psalms because the first psalm of the Psalter is a wisdom psalm and the placement of wisdom psalms at key junctures throughout the Psalter indicates that the book can be read as scripture for spiritual wisdom and instruction. Chapters 2 and 3 discuss laments because individual laments predominate in the first two books of the Psalter and community laments are important in the third book. Chapters 4, 5, and 6 discuss hymns because they are the second most prominent genre in the Psalter after laments, and because they shape the narrative direction and conclusion to the Psalter. *The Green Psalter* will show that, read as teachings, the Psalter takes the reader on a spiritual journey from injustice and alienation toward integration into creation.

CHAPTER 1

"Like A Tree Planted"[1]

WISDOM PSALMS

C anonical critics have pointed out that Psalms 1 and 2 form an introduction that provides the final editors' suggestion for how to use and understand the Psalter. There is some debate about whether Psalm 2 should be included with Psalm 1 as part of the introduction, but Gerald H. Wilson has shown evidence of "editorial manipulation" in psalms without superscriptions,[2] and neither of these psalms has a superscription. In addition, the beatitude at the beginning of Psalm 1, "Happy are those who do not follow the advice of the wicked (1:1)," and another beatitude at the end of Psalm 2, "Happy are all who take refuge in him (2:12)," create a wisdom bracket around both psalms that binds them together.

This is the first of a number of signs of wisdom influence on the final edition of the Psalter. A number of other wisdom psalms appear throughout the Psalter (Psalms 1, 19, 36, 37, 49, 73, 91, 112, 119, 127, 128, 133). Wilson sees the placement of royal psalms at editorial seams of the first three books and the placement of psalms with wisdom influences at editorial seams in the fourth and fifth books, which were added later, as evidence of wisdom influence on the final editing of the Psalter.[3] A number of these wisdom psalms emphasize *torah*, "teaching" (Pss 1, 19, 119). Claus Westermann thinks Psalms 1 and 119 may have formed the beginning and end of an earlier form of the book of Psalms.[4] Even in the present form of the Psalter, Psalm 119 is such a lengthy psalm that, as Wilson notes, its presence still dominates the final book.[5] James L. Mays identifies torah themes in a number of other psalms and portions of psalms (Psalms 18, 25, 33, 78, 89, 93, 94, 103, 105, 111, 112, 147, 148).[6] This means that the final form of the Psalter has an emphasis on wisdom and torah.

Psalm 1 is a wisdom psalm. The primary representatives of wisdom literature generally in the Hebrew Bible are Proverbs, Job, and Ecclesiastes. Wisdom psalms are characterized by the language, forms of speech, and concepts of wisdom literature.[7] Psalm 1, for instance, begins with a beatitude, "Happy are . . . (see, by comparison, Prov 3:13, 8:32), and contains wisdom topics—the study of torah and the fate of the wicked and the righteous (see, by way of comparison, Prov 10:3, 6, 7; Sir 6:37). Following Hermann Gunkel, many form critics have thought wisdom psalms were written and used in scribal schools for educational purposes.[8] However, Erhard S. Gerstenberger thinks, based on the suggestions of a number of scholars, that they were composed for use in exilic and postexilic synagogue services for "communal, liturgical instruction."[9]

J. Clinton McCann has pointed out that the language used in many English translations of Psalm 1 may not make it very appealing to modern readers. The translation of the Hebrew word *torah* as "law" may smack of legalism.[10] In this relation, the translation "righteous" may be too easily associated with self-righteousness, so that modern, English readers may incorrectly hear the psalm recommending a self-righteous, legalistic life. But this, of course, would be a misunderstanding of the psalm. The Hebrew word *torah* has a much broader meaning than "law." It can also refer to a parent's instruction to a child (Prov 28:7), and, in the Psalter, God's teaching is cosmic in scope (Psalm 19).[11] So the word *torah* is better translated "instruction" or "teaching." Similarly, "the righteous" could also be translated "the just," and I sometimes refer to them as "the just" because the Psalms connect them with care for the poor (Ps 112:9).

For Jews, the Torah of Moses is the first five books of the Bible—Genesis through Deuteronomy. The Psalter is divided into five books by doxologies at 41:31, 72:19, 89:52, and 106:48:

Book I   Psalms 1–41

Book II   Psalm 42–72

Book III   Psalm 73–89

Book IV   Psalm 90–106

Book V   Psalms 107–150

The recognition of these five books is quite ancient. The *Midrash Tehillim* states, "As Moses gave five books of laws to Israel, so David gave five books of Psalms to Israel."[12] At one time, it was common for biblical scholars to suggest that these divisions were insignificant for interpreting the Psalter because they were secondary, created long after the Psalms became a book. But Wilson showed that, in addition to the doxologies, genre designations, names in the superscriptions, and psalms without superscriptions were all evidence of editorial shaping of the Psalter.[13] Therefore, editors have arranged the Psalter into five books so that they have become the Torah of David.

Psalm 1 repeats the word *torah*, "instruction," twice in verse 2 and uses the word "meditate," which could also be translated "study." This serves to introduce the Psalter, not just as a series of hymns or prayers for communal worship, but as sacred scripture for individual

meditation and study. Regardless of the fact that the Psalms originated as the response of faithful persons to God, they are now to
be understood also as God's word to the faithful."[14] They are recom-
mended as God's words and guide to personal fulfillment and relationship with God.

The Wicked and Righteous

Psalm 1 contains two metaphors and two groups of characters that
are part of the implied narrative of wisdom psalms and wisdom literature, generally. Appearing as they do in the introduction and peri-
odically throughout the Psalter, they also contribute to the story of
the Psalter. The two metaphors are *path* and *tree,* and the characters
are the *righteous* and the *wicked.*

The wicked and the righteous appear frequently in wisdom psalms.
The descriptions of their characters, speech, behavior, and fates contrast. The wicked are insolent, arrogant, angry, and proud. They "trust
in their wealth . . . boast in the abundance of their riches" (Ps 49:6).
"Pride is their necklace; violence covers them like a garment" (73:6).
The just revere God and delight in God's commandments (112:1). They
refrain from anger, are "gracious, merciful, and," of course, "righteous"
(112:4). They are generous and give to the poor (112:5, 9).

Their speech is often mentioned and creates a contrast. The
wicked "flatter themselves" (Ps 36:2) and speak words of "mischief
and deceit" (Ps 36:3). "They scoff and speak with malice; loftily they
threaten oppression. They set their mouths against heaven, and their
tongues range over the earth. . . . They say, 'How can God know?'"
(Ps 73:8-11). By contrast, the righteous speak "wisdom," "understanding," and "justice" (Pss 37:30; 49:3).

The behavior of the wicked also contrasts with that of the just.
"The wicked plot against the righteous" (Ps 37:12; see, by way of

comparison, Ps 119:23). They use violence against the poor and needy, and those "who walk uprightly" (Ps 37:14). They taunt (119:42), deride (119:51), smear with lies (119:69), persecute the just (49:5; 119:86-87, 150, 161), "lie in wait to destroy" (119:95), and lay a snare (119:110). They seek to kill the just (37:14, 32). The just, however, spent their time studying God's teachings (Ps 119) and give generously (112:5) to the poor.

Obviously the just are acquainted with suffering, but they also confess that they are protected by God. They need not fear war, famine, disease, or any other evil (Pss 37:19; 91:5, 6, 10). God saves and rescues the righteous (37:40; 119:134).

The just are in danger of envying the success and prosperity of the wicked (Pss 37:1; 73:3) but are enjoined to trust in God (37:5) and "wait patiently" (37:7). They come to realize that the presence of God is the only reward they need and desire (73:23-24), and God's teachings are "better to [them] than thousands of gold and silver pieces" (119:72).

Different wisdom psalms seem to take different positions on a theology of retribution, and Psalm 73 may be the midpoint in a shift towards a more nuanced understanding of retribution, as some have suggested,[15] but all share a sense that God should reward the just and punish the wicked.

The just have a different destiny than the wicked. The just will be prosperous and "inherit the land" (Pss 37:11, 22, 29, 34; 112:2). They will have many children, long life (128:6), and be remembered with enduring honor (112:9; 119:6). The wicked will have their children cut off, and they will vanish leaving no posterity. They are "appointed for Sheol; Death shall be their shepherd; straight to the grave they descend" (49:14).

Much could be said, and has been said, about the realism and ethics of this way of framing the world. For the moment, the point is that there is an implied narrative in the genre. The implied narrative goes something like this: The wicked are boastful and arrogant and rely on their wealth. They persecute and seek to entrap and kill the just. They will die in dishonor and be forgotten. The just, however, trust in God and spend their time studying and meditating on God's teachings. They are generous, just, and give to the poor. They will live a long and prosperous life, have many children, and, when they die, their name will be remembered and honored. Some of these psalms (Psalms 49, 73) acknowledge that the wicked do not always get their just reward, and the just may be at risk of becoming envious, but ultimately the teaching and presence of God are their reward.

Two Paths

Psalm 1 has a concentric structure[16] that emphasizes two images—path and tree. It begins with the line: "Happy is the one who has not walked . . . on the *path* of sinners" (verse 1; author translation). The word translated "path" (*derekh*) is a common word in Hebrew that could also be translated "road" or "way." The psalm ends with the line: "the LORD watches over the *way* of the righteous, but the *way* of the wicked will perish" (verse 6; author emphasis). The word translated "way" is the same Hebrew word that was translated "path" in verse 1, so vocabulary makes clear that the metaphor of a path brackets the psalm. The metaphor is emphasized by repetition of the same vocabulary in the first verse and twice in the last verse. The metaphor is typical of wisdom literature generally, and the word translated "way" appears frequently in wisdom psalms.[17] Although the word "way" does not appear in Psalm 73, it has a related metaphor: "But as for me, my feet had almost stumbled; my steps had nearly slipped" (verse 2).

This metaphor contributes to the story of wisdom psalms and, because of their prominence in the Psalter, of the whole Psalter.

Wisdom psalms imply a story of the wicked and the just on different journeys. The Psalter is introduced as instruction on the correct path for the just person.

The metaphor of a path or journey for the life of faith has deep associations. The practice of taking religious pilgrimages is ancient and widespread. Jews, Christians, and Muslims for centuries have taken pilgrimages to Jerusalem, Mecca, or other holy sites. Many Christians reenact or mediate on the way of the cross. Much religious literature portrays the life of faith as a journey, pilgrimage, or sojourn, and the metaphor is common in secular literature. One can think of many novels and movies that are structured around a real or metaphorical journey. Thus, for contemporary readers, this metaphor may have a broad matrix of cultural associations that will give it meaning.

By emphasizing this metaphor, Psalm 1 indicates to the reader who begins the study of the Psalter as sacred scripture that they are beginning a pilgrimage.

A Tree

In the center of Psalm 1 are two agricultural metaphors for two characters and their journeys. The just are a tree, and the wicked are chaff. The mention of chaff is brief, reflecting the transience of the life of the wicked. In contrast to the deeply rooted and productive just person, the wicked are "like chaff that the wind drives away" (verse 4). Similar metaphors for the wicked appear several other times in wisdom psalms. They are "dross" (Ps 119:119) or "like smoke they vanish away" (Ps 37:20).

The relative length of the description of the tree gives it weight, and its central location in the concentric structure sets it off like a jewel in a fine setting. William Brown provides extensive documentation of the tree's rich literary and mythological associations within ancient Near Eastern cultures.[18] The tree is often associated with goddesses. Goddesses are often pictured with trees, or trees are used to symbolize goddesses.[19] The tree symbolizes wisdom, fertility, prosperity, and abundant life.[20] Dexter Callender has shown that temples often have garden precincts with sacred trees or architecture and art that depicts gardens with trees so that the garden is an "archetype of the temple."[21] Within Israel, Solomon's temple had carvings of plants and palm trees, and the two massive pillars at the entry to the temple were decorated with palms trees.[22]

Similar symbolic associations are present within the Bible. Since gardens are symbolic of the temple, and Eden is a garden planted by God in which God walks and talks with humans, the tree in Psalm 1 has associations with the temple and the presence of divinity. There is some debate in the history of interpretation about whether the "tree of life" (Gen 2:9) and the "tree of the knowledge of good and evil" (Gen 2:17) in Genesis are one or two trees. If they are understood as two trees, then Genesis has divided what was usually one tree in the ancient Near East.

Wisdom is normally associated with life. Whether the tree in Genesis 2–3 is one or two is not important in terms of literary allusion because the tree in Psalm 1 can allude to both. The "knowledge of good and evil" has at its core the ability to discern good and evil, a key element of being wise. The tree is a metaphor for both wisdom and life in the book of Proverbs, which says of woman wisdom: "She is a tree of life to those who lay hold of her; those who hold her fast are called happy" (Prov 3:18). These associations with wisdom and life fit with the context of Psalm 1 where the just are portrayed as seeking wisdom and delighting in God's teaching, and the tree is a picture of fertility and life.

The metaphor of the righteous being "like trees planted by streams of water" (Ps 1:3) introduces two metaphors that will flow through other genres in the Psalter and generate a myriad of literal and symbolic associations. The righteous will again be compared to a "green olive tree" (52:8) or a "palm tree" (92:12) and their children to "olive shoots" (128:3). And the tree has other associations. The "oaks whirl" at the approach of God (29:9) and God strikes the trees of Egypt (105:33). God also provides for trees (104:16), which in turn provide a home for the stork (104:17).

Water is almost as common in the Psalter as it is in life and creates numerous literal and metaphorical associations. Water is part of an extended metaphor for God that will be discussed at greater length in the next chapter. By way of preview, God appears accompanied by "clouds dark with water" (Ps 18:11), which pour out water (77:17). The "voice of the Lord is over the waters" (29:3). The storm provides water for the land. God makes "the waters flow" (147:18) providing water for Earth (65:9, 10) and mountains (104:13). Yet God can also bring drought and turn "springs of water into thirsty ground" (107:33).

As well as being necessary for life, too much water can be threatening. It can be described as "mighty waters" (Ps 32:6) that "roar and foam" (46:3). God may use it to judge Israel's enemies (106:11). The psalmist may complain that "waters have come up to my neck . . . deep waters." (69:1, 2, 14). Elsewhere God has pulled the psalmist out of "mighty waters" (18:16).

These references to water may be associated with references to exodus and God as Creator. God "broke the heads of the dragons in the waters" (Ps 74:13) and "gathered the waters of the sea as in a bottle; . . . the deeps in storehouses" (33:7). The waters are afraid of God (77:16), God's way is "through the might waters" (77:19), and God makes "the waters stand like a heap" (78:13). Thus the God of the exodus is the God "who spread out the earth on the waters" (136:6).

While all of the above references to water may in varying degree allude to an extended metaphor for God that will be discussed in the next chapter, there are yet other types of reference to God. There are repeated references to God bringing water from rock (Pss 78:20; 105:41; 114:8). Water may represent the presence or absence of God as when the psalmist says "my soul thirsts for you, as in a . . . land with no water" (63:1) or God "leads me beside still waters" (23:2). By the end of the Psalter, all these waters come to praise God (148:4). This does not exhaust the references to water in the Psalter, but gives an indication of the way that two metaphors, tree and water, which appear at the entryway to the Psalter in Psalm 1, run through it and support an abundant growth of literary connections and associations.

Since trees are associated with goddesses and the temple, the identification of the just person with the tree identifies the just person with divinity and the sacred. Brown claims the use of a tree as a metaphor for the blessed person denies the associations with the goddess,[23] but readers cannot be forced to read metaphors in only one direction. Denying the association with the goddess serves to maintain dualisms between male and female and God and humanity, which may be important in some theologies and dominant forms of western culture but is not necessarily biblical. Genesis 2–3 blurs the dualism of God and humanity when God says, after the humans have eaten of the tree: "[they have] become like one of us" (Gen 3:22). For an ecological reading, it is important to overcome the dualisms that have legitimated exploitation and recognize a metaphor that, in some sense, identifies humanity with divinity.

For the same reason, it is important to recognize that the metaphor simultaneously identifies the just with Earth. To deny this possibility would be to maintain the western dualisms between God and nature, God and humanity, humanity and nature, which have legitimated exploitation of Earth. The tree metaphor overcomes western dualisms by identifying God, humanity, and Earth. The tree symbolizes humanity's interrelationship and interdependence with God and Earth. Humanity, like the tree, is dependent on Earth and water for life, and Earth is sacred.

The presence of this creation metaphor standing at the center of Psalm 1 means that the Psalter as the Torah of David begins with creation like the Torah of Moses does. In the case of the Torah of David, the creation imagery focuses on the individual, one of several indications that the Psalter is to be read as the journey of a person of faith.

Destination

A path implies a destination or goal, but Psalm 1 only hints at the final destination of the reader. Brown thinks that, in the topography of the Psalter, the destination of the journey is "refuge."[24] This is true in as much as "refuge" is one of a series of interrelated metaphors that speaks of the presence and protection of God. But, in terms of the narrative movement of the Psalter, "refuge" occurs most often in individual laments and, thus, is far more frequent in the first two books of the Psalter. Within the story of the Psalter, other images that become more frequent toward the end of the Psalter will come to describe the destiny of the just.

Within the logic of Psalm 1, the destiny of the just is hinted at in the metaphor of the tree. The tree symbolizes the abundant life that is the result of an intimate relationship with both creation and the Creator. This creation image at the entry to the Psalter hints at the ultimate destiny of the faithful and climax of the Psalter, but, again, that destination will be elaborated with other metaphors as the reader journeys through the Psalter.

"You Save Humans and Animals Alike"[25]

Could the implied story of wisdom psalms or the metaphor of a tree standing at the threshold of the Psalter inspire an ecological vision of the future? The metaphor of the tree refers to creation, but Norman Habel has pointed out that creation is not necessarily ecological. Walter Zimmerli has argued that "wisdom thinks resolutely within the framework of a theology of creation."[26] However, Habel argues that the proverbs in Proverbs 10–24 may be "down to earth," but "they are anthropocentric, focusing in the needs and aspirations of humans."[27]

The wisdom psalms pose some problems for an ecological interpretation of the Psalter. The implied narrative is anthropocentric. The typical story of the wisdom psalms is about wicked and righteous human beings and their fate. Individual psalms have few references to creation, and references to animals and Earth tend to be negative. In Psalm 73, God is in heaven, and there is nothing the psalmist desires on Earth (verse 25). Other parts of Earth community seldom come into view. When they do, the references may reflect or support the low status of animals. The psalmist says of his envy and lack of understanding of the fate of the wicked:

> I was stupid and ignorant;
> > I was like a brute beast toward you. (Ps 73:22)

Elsewhere, God's protection justifies violence against dangerous creatures:

> You will tread on the lion and the adder,
> > the young lion and the serpent you will trample under foot.
> > (Ps 91:13)

Another reference that occurs twice in Psalm 49 could be understood in a couple of different ways:

> Mortals cannot abide in their pomp; . . .
>> they are like the animals that perish. (verses 12, 20)

These verses could, like Psalm 73, reflect a hierarchical view of the world with God above, animals below, and humans somewhere in between. Or it could recognize the equality of animals and humans and the fragility of their lives.

Occasionally, humans or God are compared to other parts of creation. In addition to the already mentioned comparison of the just to a tree in Psalm 1, the wicked are compared to grass and the cedars of Lebanon in Psalm 37:

> For they will soon fade like the grass,
>> and wither like the green herb. (verse 2)

> I have seen the wicked oppressing,
>> and towering like a cedar of Lebanon. (verse 35)

Psalm 128 describes the good fortune of the faithful in a way that assumes male writers and readers:

> Your wife will be like a fruitful vine within your house;
>> your children will be like olive shoots around your table.
>>> (verse 3)

On the one hand, these references may be fairly anthropocentric in as much as examples from nature are used to make a point about human beings. On the other hand, these references to humans as trees, grass, and vine, may be ecologically useful for thinking about humans as part of nature, dependent on water and Earth to flourish, interconnected with and dependent on all creation.

The wisdom psalms contain several references to God's wings. Ancient Near Eastern iconography includes pictures of gods with wings protecting worshippers.[28] This metaphor has potential for ecological reflection because it blurs western culture's dualism between God and animals. Not just humans, but also animals, are worthy of being metaphors for God, share some divine characteristics, and, thus, have intrinsic value.

Perhaps, however, a whole genre and tradition should not be painted with one brush. There is one passage in the wisdom psalms that deserves special notice. Psalm 36 may represent an alternative view within the tradition or even the expression of assumptions not made explicit elsewhere:

> Your righteousness is like the mighty mountains,
>> your judgments are like the great deep;
>> you save humans and animals alike, O LORD. (Ps 36:6)

The salvation of animals is an example of God's justice. Thus, God's justice extends to all creatures. This is a lone occurrence in wisdom psalms, but may be related to and foreshadow several similar ideas that appear several times in hymns later in the Psalter and will be discussed in subsequent chapters.

In summary, this chapter has shown that wisdom psalms have a typical narrative about the fate of the wicked and the just symbolized by the metaphor of two different journeys. This story influences the story of the Psalter because the final editors have inserted wisdom psalms and psalms with wisdom influences throughout the Psalter. In particular, Psalm 1 introduces the Psalter as "teaching" for study that will take the reader on a journey of faith.

One of the reasons for examining the typical metaphors and plot lines of genres is to begin to understand the *ethos* they create and think critically about the way they inform moral and ethical thinking, and comments above have suggested such an analysis in the area of ecological ethics. In the area of personal ethics, Sandra Siha told me recently about her work as a spiritual caregiver in a prison. She talked about the advice she gave to women who were preparing to leave prison. She and the women with whom she works are Aboriginal, and the metaphor of a path or road is part of Aboriginal spirituality in this geographical area. Her advice used the metaphor of a path and the need to be careful about what path the women's choices would take them down. She told of one woman who responded that she did not have to worry when she got out of prison because her boyfriend would take care of her. Sandra knew her boyfriend was a gang member and drug dealer. It was with great sorrow that she told me that the woman was killed shortly after being released from prison. The metaphor of different paths leading to different destinations undoubtedly has its limitations, but this example spoke to me of the power of the metaphor to describe the choices people make and their ultimate destinations.

CHAPTER 2

"God, My Rock"[1]
INDIVIDUAL LAMENTS

I n 1995, I was teaching at Pacific Theological College in the South Pacific. That year, Jacques Chirac announced that France would conduct further nuclear tests in French Polynesia. The Pacific Conference of Churches and most mainline churches of the South Pacific publicly protested against nuclear testing, and many supported decolonization. Britain, France, and the United States had all tested nuclear weapons in their colonies, and only France had not yet agreed to stop. In the same year, we took our first child and our Maohi Nui (French Polynesian) neighbors' children to see Disney's *The Lion King*.[2] The movie opens with the birth of a son to the king. The young Simba lives an idyllic life on Pride Rock until his uncle Scar conspires to have the king killed and tricks Simba into thinking he has killed his father. In shame, Simba flees into exile where he is befriended by Timon and Pumba. (I was made aware of our cultural context when the biggest laughs from the Polynesian children during the movie came when Timon and Pumba did a Hula dance.) In the meantime, Scar assumes the throne with the help of hyenas, and the savanna is consumed by drought and famine. Simba is eventually convinced by his childhood friend Nala to return to Pride Rock, defeats his uncle, and becomes king. The savanna rejoices and turns green and fertile again.

My role as a new parent and the context may have made me particularly sensitive to the role of movies in promoting cultural values. As an environmentalist, I noticed the linking of social order and ecological well being but was suspicious of the type of social order being portrayed. I wondered why a movie produced for children by a country with a long history of democracy would reproduce a monarchical social order. Nala is a strong female character, but otherwise the major characters are male, and the portrayal of gender roles is sexist and patriarchal. The dark coloring of Scar and the hyenas, the representatives of evil in the movie, and the use of African American voices, seemed to reproduce racism. Finally, as a biblical scholar, I was surprised to recognize a mythic pattern similar to one that biblical scholars have identified in the Psalms.

This chapter will discuss the social and ecological functions of this mythic pattern, which lives on in contemporary culture, and show that it is characteristic of individual laments in the Psalter. I begin with individual laments because individual laments predominate in the first two books of the Psalter and, thus, lend their imagery and implied narrative to these books. Many of these psalms have superscriptions that relate them to incidents in the life of David. They tend to refer to incidents in David's personal, rather than political, life so that David becomes the paradigmatic person of faith.[3] David becomes the reader's guide on a journey through the life of faith and, as will become evident, the recurring images and implied narrative of the individual lament construct that faith.

Genre[4]

Individual laments are the most frequently occurring genre in the Psalter,[5] especially in the earlier parts of the Psalter. The most common elements of the individual lament that are identified by genre critics are:

1. *Address and Introductory Cry for Help*: "O Lord, how many are my foes!" (Ps 3:1a); "O Lord, do not rebuke me" (6:1); "O Lord my God . . . save me" (7:1); "Why, O Lord, do you stand far off?" (10:1); "How long, O Lord? Will you forget me forever?" (13:1); "Hear a just cause, O Lord" (17:1); "My God, my God, why have you forsaken me?" (22:1a); "To you, O Lord, I lift up my soul . . . do not let me be put to shame" (25:1-2); "Vindicate me, O Lord" (26:1); "To you, O Lord, I call" (28:1); "Hear, O Lord, when I cry aloud, be gracious . . . and answer me! . . . Your face, Lord, do I seek" (27:7-8); "In you, O Lord, I seek refuge" (31:1); "Contend, O Lord, with those who contend with me" (35:1); "Hear my prayer, O Lord" (102:1); "With my voice I cry to the Lord" (142:1a).

2. *Complaint*: "How many are my foes! . . . Many . . . are saying to me, 'There is no help for you in God'" (Ps 3:1-2); "How long, you people, shall my honor suffer shame?" (4:2); "I am languishing . . . my bones are shaking with terror . . . My soul also is struck with terror . . . O Lord—how long?" (6:2-3); "Like a lion they will tear me apart; they will drag me away, with no one to rescue . . . See how they conceive evil, . . . and bring forth lies" (7:2, 14); "In arrogance the wicked persecute the poor" (10:2); "How long must I bear pain in my soul . . . ? How long shall my enemy be exalted over me?" (13:2); "O my God, I cry by day, but you do not answer; and by night, but find no rest . . . But I am a worm . . . scorned by others . . . Many bulls encircle me . . . like a ravening and roaring lion . . . you lay me in the dust of death" (22:26, 12-15); "I am in distress;

. . . my strength fails because of my misery, and my bones waste away. I am the scorn of all my adversaries, a horror to my neighbors, . . . I hear the whispering of many—terror all around! . . . as they plot to take my life" (31:9-11, 13); "For without cause they hid their net for me; without cause they dug a pit for my life. . . . Malicious witnesses rise up . . . They repay me evil for good; my soul is forlorn. . . . at my stumbling they gathered in glee. . . . they impiously mocked more and more, gnashing at me with their teeth. . . . For they do not speak peace, but they conceive deceitful words against those who are quiet in the land" (35:7, 11-12, 15-16, 20); "My days pass away like smoke. . . . All day long my enemies taunt me. . . . you have lifted me up and thrown me aside" (102:3, 8, 10); "they have hidden a trap for me. . . . no one cares for me" (142:3-4).

3. *Confession of Trust:*[6] "But you, O LORD, are a shield around me. . . . the LORD sustains me. . . . I am not afraid of ten thousands of people" (Ps 3:3, 5-6); "But know that the LORD has set apart the faithful for himself; the LORD hears when I call to him" (4:3); "But I, through the abundance of your steadfast love, will enter your house" (5:7); "The LORD judges the peoples. . . . God is my shield, who saves the upright in heart. God is a righteous judge" (7:8, 10-11); "But you do see! . . . you have been the helper of the orphan. . . . The LORD is king forever and ever . . . you will hear the desire of the meek . . . to do justice for the orphan and the oppressed" (10:14, 16a, 17a, 18a); "But I trusted in your steadfast love" (13:5); "As for me, I shall behold your face in righteousness" (17:15); "Yet you are holy, enthroned on the praises of Israel. In you our ancestors trusted; they trusted, and you delivered them. . . . Yet it was you who took me from the womb; you kept me safe on my mother's breast" (22:3-4, 9); "Good and upright is the LORD; therefore he instructs sinners in the way" (25:8); "The LORD is my strength and my shield. . . . he is the saving refuge of his anointed" (28:7-8); "But I trust in you, O LORD; I say, 'You are my

God.' My times are in your hand. . . . O how abundant is your goodness that you have laid up for those who fear you. . . . In the shelter of your presence you hide them from human plots. . . . The LORD preserves the faithful" (31:14-15, 19-20, 23).

4. *Plea or Petition:* "Rise up, O LORD! Deliver me" (Ps 3:7); "Answer me when I call" (4:1); "Be gracious to me. . . . heal me. . . . Turn, O LORD, save my life; deliver me" (6:2, 4); "Rise up, O LORD. . . . awake, O my God" (7:6); "Rise up, O LORD; O God, lift up your hand; do not forget the oppressed" (10:12); "Consider and answer me. . . . Give light to my eyes" (13:3); "From you let my vindication come. . . . incline your ear to me, hear my words. Wondrously show your steadfast love. . . . Guard me as the apple of the eye; hide me in the shadow of your wings. . . . Rise up, O LORD, confront them, overthrow them! By your sword deliver my life from the wicked" (17:2a, 6b, 7a, 8, 13); "Do not be far from me. . . . But you, O LORD, do not be far away!" (22:11a, 19); "do not let me be put to shame. . . . Make me to know your ways. . . . Turn to me and be gracious to me. . . . Relieve the troubles of my heart, and bring me out of my distress. . . . Consider my affliction and my trouble, and forgive all my sins. . . . O guard my life, and deliver me; do not let me be put to shame. . . . Redeem Israel, O God, out of all its troubles" (25:2, 4, 6, 16-18, 20, 22); "Prove me . . . and try me; test my heart and mind. . . . Do not sweep me away with sinners. . . . redeem me, and be gracious to me" (26:2, 9a, 11b); "Hear the voice of my supplication. . . . Do not drag me away with the wicked. . . . O save your people, and bless your heritage; be their shepherd, and carry them forever" (28:2a, 3a, 9); "In your righteousness deliver me. Incline your ear to me; rescue me speedily. Be a rock of refuge for me, a strong fortress to save me. . . . lead me and guide me, take me out of the net that is hidden for me. . . . Be gracious to me, O LORD. . . . deliver me from the hand of my enemies and persecutors. . . . Let your face shine upon your servant; save me in your steadfast

love. . . . Do not let me be put to shame" (31:1-2, 3b-4a, 9a, 15b-17a); "Do not be silent! O Lord, do not be far from me! Wake up! Bestir yourself for my defense, for my cause, my God and my Lord! Vindicate me" (35:22b-24a).

5. *Vow of Praise:* "I will give to the LORD the thanks due to his righteousness, and sing praise to the name of the LORD, the Most High" (Ps 7:17); "My heart shall rejoice in your salvation. I will sing to the LORD" (13:5b-6a). "From you comes my praise in the great congregation; my vows I will pay before those who fear him" (22:25); "In the great congregation I will bless the LORD" (26:12); "I will exult and rejoice in your steadfast love, because you have seen my affliction; . . . and have not delivered me into the hand of the enemy; you have set my feet in a broad place" (31:7-8); "Then I will thank you in the great congregation. . . . Then my tongue shall tell of your righteousness and of your praise all day long" (35:18, 28).

Some of the individual laments shift rather abruptly from lament to praise of God.[7] Some time ago, Joachim Begrich suggested that a priest or prophet gave an oracle of salvation at this point when they were used in the temple.[8] In addition, Westermann suggests that the worshipper experiences a real change. Their existential situation is transformed by having been heard by God: "Blessed be the LORD, for he has heard the sound of my pleadings" (Ps 28:6).[9] In other cases, the psalmist gives thanks because God has intervened in the situation. In cases where the petition has been heard or has been answered, the following elements may be part of the genre:

6. *Acknowledgement of Divine Response:* "You have put gladness in my heart more than when their grain and wine abound" (Ps 4:7); "The LORD has heard my supplication, the LORD accepts my prayer" (6:9); "Blessed be the LORD, for he has heard the sound of my pleadings" (28:6); "Blessed be the LORD, for he has wondrously shown his

steadfast love to me when I was beset as a city under siege . . . you heard my supplications when I cried out to you for help" (31:21-22).

7. *Hymnic Elements and Blessings:* "Deliverance belongs to the LORD; may your blessing be on your people!" (Ps 3:8); "I will give to the LORD the thanks due to his righteousness, and sing praise to the name of the LORD, the Most High" (7:17); "because [God] has dealt bountifully with me" (13:6b); "You who fear the LORD, praise him! . . . in awe of him, all you offspring of Israel! For he did not despise or abhor the affliction of the afflicted . . . , but heard when I cried to him" (22:23-24).

Individual scholars have recognized other recurring elements either within these categories or in addition to them. Westermann notes that the pleas of petitions may be of two types, petitions for God to hear and be present, or petitions for God to act or intervene. The psalmists may pray for their own restoration and well-being and against the prosperity and well-being of the enemies, which Westermann calls a "double wish."[10] Among the petitions, or related to them, are *imprecations against the enemies*, or prayers for evil to befall the enemies, which may be quite lengthy. Moreover, the petitions may be supported by reasons for God to act, sometimes called *motivating clauses*:[11]

8. *Imprecations against the Enemies:* "Let them fall by their own counsels; because of their many transgressions cast them out" (Ps 5:10); "All my enemies shall be ashamed and struck with terror" (6:10); "They make a pit, digging it out, and fall into the hole that they have made. Their mischief returns upon their own heads, and on their own heads their violence descends" (7:15-16); "Break the arm of the wicked and evildoers; seek out their wickedness until you find none" (10:15); "May their bellies be filled with what you have stored up for them" (17:14b); "Repay them according to their work, and according to the evil of their deeds" (28:4a); "let the wicked be put to shame;

let them go dumbfounded to Sheol. Let the lying lips be stilled that speak insolently against the righteous with pride and contempt" (31:17b-18); "Let them be put to shame and dishonor who seek after my life. Let them be turned back and confounded who devise evil against me. Let them be like chaff before the wind, with the angel of the LORD driving them on. Let their way be dark and slippery, with the angel of the LORD pursuing them. . . . Let ruin come on them unawares. And let the net that they hid ensnare them; let them fall in it—to their ruin" (35:4-6, 8); "Let all those who rejoice at my calamity be put to shame and confusion; let those who exalt themselves against me be clothed with shame and dishonor" (35:26).

9. *Motivating Clauses:* "For in death there is no remembrance of you; in Sheol who can give you praise?" (Ps 6:5); "for you are the God of my salvation; for you I wait all day long . . . for your goodness' sake, O LORD! . . . For your name's sake, O LORD . . . for I take refuge in you . . . for I wait for you" (25:5bc, 7b, 11a, 20c, 21b); "for I have walked in my integrity, and I have trusted in the LORD without wavering" (26:1); "for if you are silent to me, I shall be like those who go down to the Pit" (28:1b) "for your name's sake . . . for you are my refuge" (31:3b-4).

An Implied Narrative

This traditional description of the genre does not include the recurring imagery and implied narrative, though it may be suggested in the work of some genre critics. Westermann seems to recognize a typical story in the individual laments, even though he does not identify it in those terms. He says that among the actions of the enemy, "the most frequent and important deal with an attempt against the life of the lamenter."[12] He organizes these into several types, to which he gives the following descriptions and examples from the Psalms: "the enemy sets nets or traps" (Ps 140:4b-5), are "wild beasts" who "fall upon the lamenter" (Ps 17:11-12), or are "attacking soldiers" (7:13) or accusers in court.[13] In each case, the enemies prepare either by conspiring together and uttering threats (56:6), by surrounding the lamenter (22:12, 13, 16), or by approaching and arming themselves (27:2-3).[14] These threats on the life of the lamenter remain only a threat, but their words are "an already existing fact."[15] A number of individual laments focus on what the enemy says. Westermann says these are "characterized by two interrelated concerns: (1) The speech of the enemy seeks the destruction of the lamenter. (2) The enemy's actual intention is hidden behind lies and false friendliness."[16] This focus on what the enemy says is a step away from petition to God toward the extended descriptions of the character of the enemy that characterize many individual laments. The sheer number of such statements make them characteristic of individual laments. This "extraordinary number of assertions . . . can be gathered into two groups: a) The enemy is perverse.[17] b) The enemy is sacrilegious and godless."[18] "In contrast to the dire situation of the lamenter, the enemy is powerful, rich, always successful, never knowing want, beyond the reach of God's judgments."[19] Despite this current reality, "the future collapse of the evildoer's good fortune is predicted" (Ps 52:5-7).[20] Thus Westermann recognizes a typical drama in the individual lament. The enemies conspire together, seeking the destruction of the lamenter, though publicly their intentions may be hidden behind "lies and false friendliness."[21] They plan to set traps or attack like soldiers or wild animals. The enemies are so rich and powerful they feel beyond the judgment of God. Nevertheless, the misfortune of the lamenter will eventually be reversed, and the enemies come to ruin. This is a simple, recurring plot with stereotypical figures.

Much more work could profitably be done on this typical story in the individual laments. The following work will focus on patterns and images related to ecological justice. But before I say more about typical images and narrative patterns in the individual laments, I want to note that this narrative of wicked and righteous with associated images runs through a variety of genres and, by so doing, contributes to the understanding of the Psalter as a story of faith. Westermann thinks this polarity between the fortune of the lamenter and the fortune of the enemy is a motif that separates from the genre of lament and passes over into the separate genre of wisdom psalms (Pss 14, 36, 37, 52, 53, 58).[22] However, the influence could be in the opposite direction or a more complex relationship running in both directions. In the final form of the Psalter, however, this recurring narrative contributes to the story of faith that the Psalter tells. Psalm 1 introduces the Psalter with a contrast between the different paths of the wicked and the just. The individual laments contain lengthy descriptions of the enemies and their attacks on the lamenter. A number of wisdom psalms scattered throughout the Psalter contrast the fates of the wicked and the just. This recurring story, therefore, contributes to the faith world and story of the Psalter.

Enemies and Wild Animals

Readers of the Psalms will immediately recognize that individual laments have an implied narrative with typical characters, setting, plot, and imagery. The main characters in the story are the psalmist, the enemies, and God, and they act in typical, sometimes even stereotypical, ways.

As the discussion of the enemies has already begun to make evident, the Psalter portrays the enemies with typical imagery, some of it unique to the individual laments. In fact, the description of what the enemies do and how God should punish or repay them form recurring, stereotypical, and lengthy sections that are characteristic of laments. This hardly needs to be documented, as it will be immediately evident to those who have done much reading of the individual laments, so the discussion that follows can focus on natural imagery.

The enemies are often identified with animals; the most frequently mentioned being the lion:[23]

> Like a lion they will tear me apart;
>> they will drag me away, with no one to rescue. (Ps 7:2)

> They lurk in secret like a lion in its covert;
>> they lurk that they may seize the poor;
>> they seize the poor and drag them off in their net. (Ps 10:9)

> They are like a lion eager to tear,
>> like a young lion lurking in ambush. (Ps 17:12)

> They open wide their mouths at me,
>> like a ravening and roaring lion. . . .
> Save me from the mouth of the lion! (Ps 22:13, 21a)

> How long, O LORD, will you look on?
>> Rescue me from their ravages, my life from the lions!
>> (Ps 35:17)

> I lie down among lions that greedily devour human prey;
>> their teeth are spears and arrows, their tongues sharp swords.
>> (Ps 57:4)

This metaphorical use of the lion tends to be characteristic of individual laments. They occur eight times in individual laments in the citations above, more often than in all other genres put together. Moreover, of the five other times lions[24] appear in the psalms, four are in similar uses in the related genres: thanksgiving (34:10), communal lament (58:6), and a confession of trust (91:13). The one remaining occurrence is in a hymn (104:21). So these references to the enemies as lions are typical of individual laments.

Animals and wilderness are often a threat to human society in laments. A twice-repeated verse in Psalm 59 summarizes the dynamic:

Each evening they come back,
>howling like dogs and prowling about the city. (verses 6, 14)

"Evening" anticipates night and darkness. The dogs threaten the city, the symbol of human civilization. Since there are wild, semi-wild, and domestic dogs, they, themselves, are a symbol that mediates between nature and civilization.

In a few places, wilderness has positive rather than negative connotations. In Ps 55:6-11, the wilderness is a place of refuge from the violence and strife of the city.

"O that I had wings like a dove! I would fly away and be at
>rest;
>truly, I would flee far away;
>I would lodge in the wilderness; *Selah*
I would hurry to find a shelter for myself
>from the raging wind and tempest."
Confuse, O Lord, confound their speech;
>for I see violence and strife in the city.
Day and night they go around it on its walls,
>and iniquity and trouble are within it;
>ruin is in its midst;
>oppression and fraud do not depart from its marketplace.

These different pictures of wilderness represent mythological reflections on the relation between humanity and nature. This binary construction of civilization and wilderness, with wilderness alternatively viewed as something to be conquered or as a place of refuge and healing remains strong in contemporary society. While a positive view of wilderness provides political motivation for the contemporary environmental movement, the separation between wilderness and civilization is part of the separation between humanity and nature that provides ideological support for the exploitation of Earth.

The Divine Warrior

Biblical scholars have long noted the presence in the Hebrew Bible of a mythic pattern similar to the Mesopotamian myth *Enuma Elish* and the Ugaritic myth of the battle of Baal against Yamm or Sea. Ugarit was an ancient Canaanite city where archaeologists discovered a library of cuneiform texts that predate Israel and have close linguistic and cultural parallels to the Hebrew Bible. Among the mythological texts discovered there are stories of Baal's battle against Sea.

Psalm 74, a communal lament, is one example of the presence of this myth in the Hebrew Bible:

> Yet God my King is from of old,
>> working salvation in the earth.
> You divided the sea by your might;
>> you broke the heads of the dragons in the waters.
> You crushed the heads of Leviathan;
>> you gave him as food for the creatures of the wilderness.
>> (verses 12–14)

The Hebrew name *Leviathan* has the same root letters as the Ugaritic name *Lotan*, a sea monster. Other references to the myth are found in Pss 18:14-19; 24; 46:1-7; 68:7-10; 76; 77:15-20; 89:5-14; 104:2-9, 31-32;[25] 114:3-7. But the cultural influence goes beyond literary allusions. Frank Moore Cross and others have shown that Israel took over from Canaanite religion the mythic pattern, the *mythos* or narrative structure and images.[26]

In Mesopotamia, Ugarit, and Israel, the mythic pattern has a number of common, recurring features.[27] First, the divine warrior marches forth to battle against the forces of chaos accompanied by a storm, lightning, thunder, fire, and the shaking of Earth. Second, the god does battle with the gods and nations who threaten social and cosmic order. They respond with fear and trembling at the rebuke of the divine warrior and flee or are scattered. The first part is sometimes called a theophany,[28] an appearance of god, and the second element is often called the battle against chaos (*Chaoskampf* in German),[29] and discussed separately. But both are part of the larger mythic narrative as indicated by their frequent occurrence together in ancient Near Eastern literature and in the Bible. Third, the warrior returns to the divine mountain, takes up the kingship of the gods, and builds a temple. Fourth, the god sends word from the temple, and nature responds with fertility and joy.

What has not been recognized by biblical scholars is that this mythic pattern creates much of the narrative structure of individual laments. Much of this implied narrative is recognizable without any knowledge of the ancient Near Eastern mythic pattern.

A Narrative Pattern in Laments

The individual laments assume a valley-shaped geography and narrative structure. Spatial metaphors that create this structure are common. The psalmist is crushed to the ground, has fallen in a pit, goes down to Sheol—the Pit—sinks in mire, or a flood, and cries "out of the depths."[30]

The psalmists look up to God, who is like a mountain, on Mount Zion or in the heavens. They ask God to come down to help them and look forward to a time when they will be reconciled to God, restored to community, and give thanks on God's sacred mountain.

He looked down from his holy height,
    from heaven the LORD looked at the earth,
to hear the groans of the prisoners,
    to set free those who were doomed to die;
so that the name of the LORD may be declared in Zion,
    and his praise in Jerusalem. (Ps 102:19-21)

The future is often up because it is pictured in the temple, on Mount Zion: "let them bring me to your holy hill and to your dwelling" (Ps 43:3). The recurring metaphor of the path or way of God, though its origin is in wisdom, also contributes to the sense of narrative structure. This narrative geography is characteristic of laments.

From an ecological perspective, much of the imagery in the individual laments is disturbing. The imagery and plot is predominantly anthropocentric. God is often portrayed in anthropomorphic language and the complaints are largely limited to suffering and injustice in the human community. In Ps 102:26-27, Earth perishes, is evidently disposable, but God endures forever. The use of the divine warrior myth is ambiguous from the perspective of Earth. On the one hand, the narrative has strong associations with life and fertility in the fourth part of the pattern. On the other hand, a God from the sky battles Earth in order to deliver humanity from Earth. Small wonder that a culture fed this imagery for generations as its spiritual food would so often understand humanity as above and separate from an Earth with no intrinsic value that had to be conquered and subdued.

The Battle against Death

While biblical scholars widely agree on the presence in the Bible of imagery similar to Baal's battle against Sea, few detect evidence of

Baal's battle against Death.[31] And no one that I know of has noticed that imagery similar to Baal's battles against Death is characteristic of individual laments. Although Baal's battle against Death and Baal's battle against Sea are both divine warrior myths, there are some differences.

In the Ugaritic Myth of Baal's battle against Death, Baal comes down from his sacred mountain, dies, and goes down into the underworld. His sister Anat eventually rescues him. Death is king of the underworld, and his home is the middle of a swamp. At one point the text reads:

> Then toward the midst of his city, the Swamp,
> Muck his royal house,
> Phlegm, the land of his inheritance.[32]

Later in the story a message comes from Death to Baal:

> Now you will surely descend into the throat of El's son, Death,
> Into the watery depths of El's Darling, the Hero. . . .
> One lip to the earth, one lip to the heavens;
> He will stretch his tongue to the stars.
> Baal must enter inside him;
> He must go down into his mouth.[33]

This imagery seems to be characteristic of the individual lament. Psalm 69, an individual lament, is perhaps the most explicit example of this story line and these images in the Bible:

> Save me, O God,
>> for the waters have come up to my neck.
> I sink in deep mire, where there is no foothold;
>> I have come into deep waters, and the flood sweeps over me.
>>> (verses 1–2)

Do not let the flood sweep over me,

> or the deep *swallow* me up,

> or the Pit close its *mouth* over me. (verse 15, author emphasis)

Note that the mention of "mire" and "waters" are similar to the images of swamp and waters used of Death's home.[34] And the imagery of the Pit having a mouth and the deep swallowing the psalmist is similar to Death swallowing Baal. References to going down into the Pit, Sheol, or sinking in the watery depths are fairly frequent in other individual laments or closely related genres like individual thanksgiving. The psalmist does not want to be "like those who go down to the Pit" (Ps 28:1, 143:7), complains that God has "put me in the depths of the Pit, in the regions dark and deep" (88:6), wishes of the enemies that God would "cast them down into the lowest pit" (55:23), or "let them be flung into pits, no more to rise!" (140:10). Or the psalmist may give thanks that God "drew me up from the desolate pit, out of the miry bog" (40:2). To these could also be added references to going down to Sheol (Ps 6:5; 31:17; 55:15; 86:13; 88:3; 139:8; 141:7). It seems to me that this imagery has become a part of the English language because people say they are "down" or "in the pits" to express depression or misfortune. This ancient imagery is characteristic of individual laments.

The next chapter will show that imagery akin to the battle against Sea is characteristic of community laments. In Ugaritic literature, the battle against Sea is a battle against natural and political chaos, and the battle against Death is, as the name suggests, a battle against death and sterility. One can understand how the battle against Sea's political concern might be at home in community lament, and the battle against Death's concern with infertility and death might be at home in individual laments.

Popular Culture

What fascinates me is the way in which the divine warrior myth reappears in popular culture and seems to function as a symbolic reflection on our relationship to nature. In Disney's *The Lion King*, the movie begins on a height, Pride Rock. Simba's father is killed in a valley, trampled by a stampede of wild beasts. Simba goes into exile in the desert. Under the rule of his uncle Scar, the savanna around Pride Rock is decimated by drought and famine. Simba returns to Pride Rock, battles his uncle, who falls from Pride Rock and is eaten by the hyenas who had been his accomplices. When Simba becomes king, the savanna rejoices and turns green and fertile again. The narrative structure and images are amazingly similar to biblical scholar's descriptions of the divine warrior myth in Israel and Canaan, and an ecological concern is noticeable.

Culturally, a children's movie may seem a trivial place to note the recrudescence of the divine warrior myth. However, Karin Lesnik-Oberstein shows that:

> Ideological, political and moral issues are asserted with concentrated force with regard to the "child," and find their clearest articulation in books assigned to a child-audience in the prevalent belief (right or wrong) that these books have a unique capacity to affect, and therefore enlighten, their child-readers. The books adults produce for, or allocate to, the "child" they construct have always powerfully reflected their efforts to redeem humans and the human in the present and future, spiritually, emotionally, or morally. Environmental redemption is part of this ongoing narrative.[35]

Since John Locke and Jean Jacques Rousseau, the social constructions of nature and children have been closely connected. Children exist in a Garden of Eden state, before civilization and alienation from nature. Rousseau thought children should be taught by direct contact with nature, but, ironically, since they had to learn to read, the books they read should be about nature. Thus he had Emile read *Robinson Crusoe*.[36] Lesnik-Oberstein says that her survey of the books in the children's section of a bookstore indicated that roughly two-thirds of contemporary children's books have natural images or environmental concerns.[37] Well-known examples include *Uncle Remus, Charlotte's Web, Black Beauty, Babar the Elephant, Rupert the Bear, Winnie-the Pooh, Watership Down, Lassie-Come-Home, The Story of Doctor Doolittle, Swiss Family Robinson, The Wind in the Willows, Heidi, The Secret Garden, Tarzan of the Apes,* Little House in the Big Woods series, and *Lord of the Flies.* Animal characters that can walk and talk like human beings are a common feature in children's literature.

Many of these books have been adapted as cartoons, television series, and movies. Some have a valley-shaped plot and images similar to laments. In *Heidi*, Heidi begins in the mountains, goes down the mountain to the city to learn to read, and returns to the mountain at the end. Tolkein's book, *The Two Towers* (Lord of the Rings, II),[38] and the movie, *Lord of the Rings: The Two Towers*,[39] have images—enemies, pit, darkness, water, king, mountains—and a valley-shaped narrative structure, similar to laments, and symbolic meditations on our relationship to nature are prominent. The way in which this mythic pattern takes part in an ongoing meditation on society and nature is evident in the increase in environmental concerns in contemporary children's books and movies.

God as Rock

Mary Daly said: "If God is male, then male is God. The divine patriarch castrates women as long as he is allowed to live on in the human imagination."[40] This quote points to the power of metaphor to create reality. From the perspective of Earth, we could say: if God is human, then the human is God. The divine human destroys Earth as long as the divine human is allowed to live on in the human imagination.[41] An ecological hermeneutic, therefore, needs to find Earth metaphors for figuring reality and empowering Earth community. God as rock is one such possibility. References to God as rock are more frequent in Psalms than God as father—references to God as rock occur twenty-one times[42] and references to God as father only three times.[43]

The image of God as rock is characteristic of individual laments. It appears in a variety of genres, which may be an indication of its status as a metaphor for God, but it appears more often in individual laments (Pss 28:1; 31:2, 3; 42:9; 71:3; 94:22) than any other genre. Given the relationships between genres, it is easy to understand how an image at home in individual laments might migrate to genres that share border regions, like individual thanksgivings (Pss 18:2, 31, 46; 92:15), a psalm of trust (Ps 62:2, 6, 7), and communal laments (Pss 89:26; 144:1, 2) among others (Pss 19:14; 78:35; 95:1). Nevertheless, it appears far more often in individual laments than any other genre and, as was noted earlier, has a logical relation to the narrative pattern of the individual lament. The rock is a mountainous hideaway from enemies or the solid ground that is sought by the psalmist who is sinking in mire or drowning in the ocean. In the implied narrative, God became both the redeemer who will place the psalmist on a solid rock and, by metaphorical extension, the rock itself.

I am suspicious of some uses of rock imagery in contemporary culture. For instance, there seem to me to be many ads for cars, pickup trucks, and SUVs in which the vehicle is perched on a mountain, a cliff, or a rocky promontory on the ocean. Or the vehicle is seen scrambling over rocks, ascending a hill. As the ditty says, "Chevy trucks, like a rock."™ The imagery appeals to people's sense of alienation from

Earth and, ironically, portrays the SUV as a way to get back to nature. Most purchasers are urbanites who use these vehicles to commute and seldom, if ever, get out into the country (as if nature were not present in the city). Not only are SUVs gas guzzlers, they require the mining of minerals and huge amounts of oil to manufacture them. As is too often the case in contemporary culture, natural imagery and the way back to healing nature are coopted by the domination of nature.

Imagery and a narrative, similar to the one I described in the Psalms, seems to appear in *Lord of the Rings* and function in our society as a symbolic reflection on our relation to nature. In the movie version, the people of Rohan, faced by the much larger armies of the evil wizard Sauron, retreat into Helm's Deep, a fortress built into the wall of a cliff at the end of a valley between mountains—*rock* as refuge, fortress, stronghold, and perhaps salvation. They are saved at the last minute, but later, Aaragorn, the future king, decides to attempt the dangerous trip through tunnels in the mountain to get more help in the coming war. The trip is dangerous because the tunnels and clefts in the mountains are inhabited by ghost armies, and many have never returned. But Aaragorn manages to solicit the help of the ghost armies in the war against the forces of evil and emerges from the other side. By fighting with Aaragorn, the ghosts are released from bondage, so the story is one of redemption. Also the rock and mountain are a refuge, the place of contact with the spirit world, and the way to get help/salvation in the fight against the forces of evil.

The books reflect a romantic view of nature that developed in Europe in reaction to the industrial revolution. Earth community in the book is alive, thinks, speaks, and resists injustice. The making of the book into a Hollywood movie, at a time when North American culture is becoming more concerned about the environmental crisis, becomes on a symbolic level part of our society's search for better stories and images for the construction of nature.

In conclusion, this chapter has suggested that individual laments assume a typical story with typical characters and imagery and has focused particularly on recurring, natural imagery. The enemies are described in stereotypical language, which includes describing them as lions and other wild animals. The psalmists describe their plight as sinking into the Pit or sinking under the water. The psalmist prays to be rescued, and the assumed narrative of deliverance by God shares elements with the ancient Near Eastern pattern of the march of the divine warrior. Also characteristic of individual laments is the portrayal of God as rock. The psalmist looks forward and upward to standing firmly on a rock of refuge, or on Mount Zion in the temple with God. This typical imagery and implied narrative imagine a world that continues to influence contemporary constructions of nature. Thus, contemporary society continues to view wild animals as enemies and wilderness as both refuge and threat. The movies *The Lion King* and *Lord of the Rings* are examples of the continued use of these images and narrative patterns as contemporary reflections on society and ecology. This chapter noted imagery in individual laments from the divine warrior myth, and the next chapter will present more evidence of influence from the ancient Near Eastern myth of the divine warrior in communal laments. Whereas imagery similar to a particular version of the mythic pattern, the battle of Canaanite Baal against Death, was characteristic of individual laments, imagery similar to another version, Baal's battle against Sea, will be seen to be characteristic of communal laments. The next chapter will also show further examples of similar images and narrative patterns in contemporary stories that express a growing ecological concern in contemporary society.

CHAPTER 3

Making Peace with Leviathan

COMMUNITY LAMENTS

C ommunity laments are the most common genre in the third book of the Psalter. The third book relates the story of the slow decline and fall of the nation after the reign of Solomon, beginning with the division of the nation, a long series of coups and poor leaders, the fall of first the north and then the south, and captivity in Babylon. The second book ends with the statement: "The prayers of David son of Jesse are ended" (Ps 72:20). The final psalm in the third book, Psalm 89, ends by lamenting the breaking of God's covenant to keep a descendant of David on the throne. The superscriptions ascribe only one psalm in the third book to David. The majority are ascribed to Asaph and other priestly temple singers from the reign of David and Solomon who now lead the people in worship during these turbulent times.

This chapter begins with a brief outline of the elements of the community lament as described by genre critics. This section is brief because the description of the genre of community lament is already well known and widely available. The description of the typical narrative pattern and imagery, however, is unique to this work and therefore discussed at greater length in several subsections that discuss the typical characters, plot, the divine warrior myth, and its influence on the typical plot and reflect on the way similar narrative patterns and imagery in contemporary culture reflect and inform our relationship to nature.

Genre

The community lament in the Psalms has the following elements:[1]

1. *Address to God and Introductory Petition*: "O God, do not keep silence" (Ps 83:1a). Sometimes an introductory complaint is included "O God, why do you cast us off forever? . . . Remember your congregation. . . . Remember Mount Zion" (74:1-2); "O God, the nations have come into your inheritance" (79:1a). Praise of God may also be part of the introductory address: "Give ear, O Shepherd of Israel, you who lead Joseph like a flock! You who are enthroned upon the cherubim, shine forth" (80:1).

2. *Lament or Complaint*: "Yet you have rejected us and abased us . . ." (Ps 44:9-16; see also 44:19, 22, 24-25); "The enemy has destroyed everything in the sanctuary . . ." (74:3b-9); "They have laid Jerusalem in ruins. . . ." (79:1b-5, 7, 8c); "How long will you be angry with your people's prayers? You have fed them with the bread of tears. . . . our enemies laugh among themselves" (80:4-6); "Even now your enemies are in tumult. . . . They lay crafty plans against your people. . . ." (83:2-12). David has become "the scorn of his neighbors" (89:41). The "enemies taunt" (89:51).

3. *Expressions of Trust or Confidence:* "You are my King and my God; . . . Through you we push down our foes" (Ps 44: 4-5); "Yet God

my King is from of old, working salvation in the earth . . ." (74:12-17); "You brought a vine out of Egypt . . ." (80:8-11).

4. *Motivating Clauses:*[2] "All this has come upon us, yet we have not forgotten you, or been false to your covenant. . . . Redeem us for the sake of your steadfast love" (Ps 44:17, 26); "Answer us, so that those whom you love may be rescued" (60:5); "The enemy scoffs, and an impious people reviles your name. . . . the impious scoff at you all day long. . . . Do not forget the clamor of your foes, the uproar of your adversaries" (74:18, 22, 23); "Help us . . . for the glory of your name . . . for your name's sake. Why should the nations say, 'Where is their God?' . . . Return sevenfold . . . the taunts with which they taunted you" (79:9, 10, 12); "Have regard for this vine, the stock that your right hand planted" (80:14-15); "Those who hate you have raised their heads" (83:2).

5. *Petition:* "Rouse yourself! . . . Awake, do not cast us off forever! . . . Rise up, come to our help. Redeem us" (Ps 44:23, 26); "Do not deliver the soul of your dove to the wild animals. . . . Have regard for your covenant. . . . Rise up, O God, plead your cause" (74:19-21, 23); "Pour out your anger on the nations. . . . Do not remember against us the iniquities of our ancestors; let your compassion come speedily. . . . Help us. . . . deliver us, and forgive our sins. . . . Let the groans of the prisoners come before you. . . . Return sevenfold into the bosom of our neighbors the taunts with which they taunted you" (79:6, 8-9, 11-12); "Restore us, O God; let your face shine, that we may be saved" (80:3); "Turn again . . . look down from heaven. . . . have regard for this vine. . . . let your hand be upon the one at your right hand" (80:14, 17); "O my God, make them like whirling dust, like chaff before the wind. . . . let them perish in disgrace" (83:13-17).

6. *Promise of Praise.* "In God we have boasted continually, and we will give thanks to your name forever" (Ps 44:8); "let the poor and needy praise your name" (74:21b); "Then we your people, the flock

of your pasture, will give thanks to you forever; from generation to generation we will recount your praise" (79:13); "Give us life, and we will call on your name" (80:18); "That we may give thanks to your holy name and glory in your praise" (106:47b).

In summary, the genre of community lament is typically described by biblical scholars as having: (1) an address to God and introductory petition, (2) lament or complaint, (3) expressions of trust or confidence, (4) motivating clauses, (5) petition, and (6) promise of praise. The petition, promise of praise, and tendency to append oracles all create a future expectation that contributes to the narrative flow. This typical way of describing the genre, however, focuses on form and content. It does not discuss the typical imagery and implied narrative that is important for understanding how the genre constructs reality and influences contemporary culture. The following sections, therefore, describe the *mythos* of the community lament.

Characters

Anyone who reads the community laments in the Psalter repeatedly notices an implied narrative with typical characters, setting, plot, and imagery. The main characters in the story are the psalmist, the enemies, and God. Their portrayal tends to be stereotypical.

There are a number of similarities between the way the enemies are portrayed in community laments and in individual laments. In community laments, as in individual laments, the enemies are characterized by arrogant or deceptive speech (Ps 12:2-4). Their "mouths speak lies" (144:8, 11). They often laugh at Israel or God (74:10, 18, 22). They taunt (79:4, 12; 89:51) or say "where is their God?" (79:10). They "lay crafty plans . . ." (83:3-4). The psalmists are fed up with the "contempt" and "scorn" of those who are proud and complacent (123:3-4). The story may be told from different perspectives. The enemies sometimes are planning to attack (Ps 83), but more often have already attacked (Pss 74, 79, 80).

As in individual laments, community laments several times portray the enemies as wild animals. Psalm 58 says they have venom like a serpent and "like the deaf adder who has closed his ear" (verse 4; author translation) and ask God to "tear out the fangs of the young lions" (verse 6). Psalm 74 asks God not to "deliver the soul of your dove to the wild animals" (verse 19). In Psalm 79, the nations "have given the bodies of your servants to the birds of the air for food, the flesh of your faithful to the wild animals of the earth" (verse 2).

In community laments, the enemies are national rather than individual enemies. The enemies are other nations. In two oracles, the historical enemies of Israel are listed (Pss 60:6-9; 108:7-10). Psalm 83 lists the nations who seek to overthrow Israel—Edom, Moab, Ammon, Philistia, Tyre, and Assyria (verses 5–8). In (at least) one case, Psalm 90, no enemies are in view; the iniquities of the people, not enemies, have caused the people's problems.

In a couple of cases, the language is vague so the "wicked" could refer either to other nations or to people within the community. Psalm 58 could refer to the wicked within the community. If, however, the opening verse is God speaking in judgment on the gods of the nations, and verse ten refers to a military victory (the righteous "will bathe their feet in the blood of the wicked"), then the wicked may be other nations. The language is vague enough, however, to apply to people within the community.

God's character contrasts with that of the enemies. God is steadfast and faithful, keeping promises (Ps 12:6). God is typically portrayed as king, warrior, and judge, which are functions that are combined in the ancient Near Eastern king. Psalm 60 laments: "You do not go out, O God, with our armies" (verse 10) and expresses confidence that eventually God "will tread down our foes" (verse 12).

There is quite a bit of diversity in the way God is expected to act. Sometimes the expectation is vague. Other times it is quite specific. God's intervention as a judge and warrior is not the only possibility, but is frequent.

Aside from God as king and warrior, pastoral imagery for God and people is fairly prominent, as it is in other genres. God is a shepherd, and the people are God's flock (Pss 44:11, 74:1, 79:13).

Especially significant from the perspective of Earth are references to God as gardener and Israel as a vine. God drove out other nations and "planted" Israel (12:2). This metaphor is elaborated at some length in Psalm 80:

> You brought a vine out of Egypt;
>> you drove out the nations and planted it.
> You cleared the ground for it;
>> it took deep root and filled the land.
> The mountains were covered with its shade,
>> the mighty cedars with its branches;
> it sent out its branches to the sea,
>> and its shoots to the River.
> Why then have you broken down its walls,
>> so that all who pass along the way pluck its fruit?
> The boar from the forest ravages it,
>> and all that move in the field feed on it.
> Turn again, O God of hosts;
>> look down from heaven, and see;
>> have regard for this vine,
> the stock that your right hand planted.
> They have burned it with fire, they have cut it down;
>> may they perish at the rebuke of your countenance.
>> (verses 8–16)

On the one hand, the image of a nature modified by human work in which wild animals are treated as the enemies is not without problems from the perspective of Earth. On the other hand, pastoral imagery has been a major locus in western culture for reflection on humanity's relationship with nature[3] and may be part of the popularity of Psalm 23, and pastoral imagery is used generally for expressing our relationship with God and nature. The pastoral landscape mediates between wilderness and civilization in art and literature. Moreover, this is an image of God who is present and involved, getting hands dirty in the work of creation. The metaphor could help overcome the separation between humanity and nature by focusing on the identification of humans and nature. Nations, like plants, rely on the providential presence of God in creation in order to flourish. Like plants, people and nations are dependent on water, fertile soils, and other natural resources. Human societies are interdependent and interrelated with all of Earth community. The metaphor can speak to God's involvement in nature and history.

Plot

A number of elements of the genre create an orientation to the future that contributes to an implied narrative. A vow to praise was a common element of the individual laments in the previous chapter, but, as Claus Westermann notes, "the vow of praise is seldom met with" in the community lament.[4] He thinks the vow to praise is secondary and came over into community laments from individual laments. Among the psalms widely regarded as community laments, only one seems to have in mind something like a vow to praise (Ps 80:18). A few others use language that is similar to, or the same as, language used in individual laments. Westermann says that "where the vow of praise is lacking, the [community laments] end either with a petition or with a confession of trust."[5] It might be more accurate to say that a vow to praise at the end of the psalm may be supplemented by a petition (80:19), replaced by a petition (74:23; 89:50-52) or a confession of trust (44:26), or both (60:11-12). Although the promise of praise is a little more muted than in individual laments, there remains a movement toward praise typical of laments.

Westermann points to evidence in the prophets of community laments being answered by oracles. This is also evident in a couple of psalms that begin as lament and end with an oracle. According to Westermann, these are no longer laments but have become prophetic liturgies.[6] The important point to note for our purposes is that all these features—the promise of praise, the petitions, and the oracles—all create a movement toward the future that contributes to the implied narrative.

The implied plot is created by a tension between the psalmist's memory of the past acts of God and the current realities. Westermann notes the recalling of the saving deeds of God in the past as a typical feature of the genre.[7] The people look back to a time when "it was said among the nations, 'The LORD has done great things for them,'" and they rejoiced (Ps 126:2-3). They pray to God that those times will come again. This sets up a tension with current realities. This tension generates questions that are also typical: "How long?" These acts of God in the past create the expectation that God will act again according to the same or a similar pattern.

Another aspect of the tension that creates the typical plot is divine justice. The psalmist sees violence and injustice in the world and expects God to be on the side of peace and justice. The psalmist expects God to act on behalf of the poor and needy. In Psalm 12, God acts "'because the poor are despoiled'" (verse 5). Psalm 79 asks God to "let the groans of the prisoners come before you" (verse 11).

In terms of the distress or concern that occasions the lament and is part of the implied story, the destruction of the temple and the exile loom large (Pss 74:3b-7; 79:1). In some cases, however, the concerns are more general and vague and could have been used in a variety of periods in the history of Israel and Judah (44:9-16). David, as the representative of the community, is "the scorn of his neighbors" (Ps 89:41). God has "covered him with shame" (Ps 89:45).

There is some spatial imagery. God may be in the heavens and come down to help the people. The people may be in "deep darkness" (Ps 44:19) or in the dust or ground. Horizontal imagery is also present as God may come forth. The vertical spatial imagery was more prevalent in creating the narrative structure of the individual lament.

The vision of the future is one in which social justice is interrelated with well-being of Earth. Some translations like the NRSV translate the Hebrew word *tsedeq* in the following example and in other places in the Psalms as "righteousness," which may be misleading in English because "righteousness" often has connotations of individual morality. In the Psalms, however, the word *tsedeq* includes social conduct, and thus I have translated "justice" to bring out the way social justice and fertility are identified in Psalm 85:

Loyalty and truth will meet;
   justice and well-being kiss.
Faithfulness will sprout from Earth,
   and justice look down from the skies.
The LORD also gives what is good;
   our Earth gives her produce.
Justice will go before God,
   and will make a path for God's feet. (verses 10–13; author translation)

Divine Warrior

The divine warrior pattern influences the typical imagery and narrative of community laments. This way of portraying God is widespread in the ancient Near East, so it is not surprising that it appears in a number of genres in the Psalms. The way it is used in the community lament, however, is unique. Whereas the individual lament tended to use imagery akin to Baal's battle against Death, the community lament tends to use imagery akin to the battle against the Sea. The previous chapter described the elements of the divine warrior pattern as (1) the approach of God from the divine council accompanied by the imagery of a storm, (2) the battle with the sea, sea monsters, and the enemies of the individual or nation, (3) the return to the mountain of God where those delivered lead in the praise of God, and (4) Earth community responds with joy, praise, and fertility. Not all elements of a genre appear in every occurrence of the genre, so it is to be expected that this *mythos* will not appear in every community lament. However, the following discussion shows that the battle against the Sea appears frequently enough to be considered typical of the genre.

Experts on the genres of the Psalms vary widely on which psalms they consider community laments. Approximately eight psalms are widely recognized as community laments (Pss 44, 60, 74, 79, 80, 83, 90, 137) and ten others that some, but not all, would include among community laments (Pss 12, 58, 85, 89, 106, 108, 123, 126, 129, 144). The imagery and narrative pattern of the march of the divine warrior is obvious in five community laments (Pss 74, 83, 89, 106, 144). The first two are widely recognized as community laments, and some would include the other three. Psalm 74 remembers God's defeat of Leviathan and the resulting fertility (water) and natural order of the seasons:

Yet God my King is from of old,
>working salvation in the earth.

You divided the sea by your might;
>you broke the heads of the dragons in the waters.

You crushed the heads of Leviathan;
>you gave him as food for the creatures of the wilderness.

You cut openings for springs and torrents;
>you dried up ever-flowing streams.

Yours is the day, yours also the night;
>you established the luminaries and the sun.

You have fixed all the bounds of the earth;
>you made summer and winter. (verses 12-17)

The plea for God to act, however, remains fairly limited and vague: "Rise up, O God, plead your cause" (Ps 74:22). On the one hand, this may represent some tentativeness about the future but, on the other hand, leaves open exactly how God will act. The imagery clearly identifies the mythic pattern in Psalm 74, and it includes elements of the narrative pattern.

In Psalm 83, the enemies are in tumult (verse 2). God is asked to intervene with wind, fire (verses 13–14), and tempest and hurricane (verse 15), the metaphorical imagery of the storm theophany. The psalm ends with the nations recognizing God as "Most High over all the earth" (verse 18). So Psalm 83 contains both elements of the imagery and narrative pattern of the march of the divine warrior.

Psalms 89 and 144 are among those psalms whose inclusion as community laments might be debated by some scholars. While some distinguish these psalms on basis of their royal content, their form places them within the genre of community lament. Imagery of the divine warrior myth is clearly present in both. Psalm 89 pictures God in "the council of the holy ones" addressed as "Lord God of hosts" (verses 7–8). The saving deeds that are recalled are from the myth of the divine warrior. God rules the "raging sea" (verse 9) and crushes Rahab (verse 10). We have no references to Rahab from elsewhere in the ancient Near East, but several appearances of Rahab in similar contexts in the Bible (Job 9:13; 26:12; Isa 51:9) indicate that Rahab was one of the primordial monsters that God defeated. The battle seems to be followed by a procession and celebration (verses 15–16).

Moreover, Psalm 144, another royal lament, contains a storm theophany:

> Bow your heavens, O LORD, and come down;
>   touch the mountains so that they smoke.
> Make the lightning flash and scatter them;
>   send out your arrows and rout them.
> Stretch out your hand from on high;
>   set me free and rescue me from the mighty waters,
>   from the hand of aliens. (verses 5–7)

The enemies of Israel are understood in mythic terms as mighty waters, and, true to the mythic pattern, God's intervention is followed by praise (verse 9) and blessing and fertility (verses 12–15). Both Psalms 89 and 144, therefore, clearly follow the mythic pattern.

Psalm 106, a mixed form, or late community lament influenced by Deuteronomistic theology, could perhaps be mentioned here, because it has similarities to individual and community laments. In Psalm 106, the remembrance of saving deeds of the past and confession has turned into a long recitation of the history of Israel. Part of the similarity to community laments is the recollection of saving deeds in verses 8-12. These verses are a mythological interpretation of the exodus. God "rebuked"[8] the Red Sea (Ps 106:9). The Hebrew word translated "rebuked" appears frequently in the context of the storm theophany in the Hebrew Bible,[9] and the same word is used in the Ugaritic language for Baal's "rebuke" of the council of gods for being afraid of the messengers of Sea.[10] The mythic dimensions of the event are evident in the parallel between Red Sea and "the deep" (verse 9). Mythic allusions may be present in Earth swallowing Dathan and Abiram, and fire and flame burning the wicked (verses 17–18). The psalm ends with the anticipation of praise (verse 47). Psalm 106, therefore, combines features of individual and community laments and describes God's actions according to the mythic pattern.

Although mythological imagery is not as explicit as in the above psalms (74, 83, 89, 106, 144), several psalms, which are widely recognized as community laments, show evidence that the imagery is assumed, and several others have elements of the narrative pattern. In Psalm 44, the image of God that lies behind the psalm is clearly of God as a warrior:

> You are my King and my God;
>> you command victories for Jacob.
> Through you we push down our foes;
>> through your name we tread down our assailants.
>> (verses 4–5)

As in the typical pattern, the enemies make fun of them (verses 13–16), and there is a movement toward praise: "We will give thanks to your name forever" (verse 8). As might be expected, there is some overlap in narrative and imagery between the community lament and individual lament. Thus, wild animals, in this case jackals, appear as enemies, and the psalmists are in "deep darkness" (verse 19), "sink down to the dust," and their bodies "cling to the ground" (verse 25).

In Psalm 60, God has caused the land to quake and totter (verse 2), imagery common in the march of the divine warrior (Judg 5:4; 2 Sam 22:8 par. Ps 18:7; 68:8; 77:18; Nah 1:5). God is clearly addressed as a divine warrior who fights on behalf of Israel. The psalmist complains, "You do not go out, O God, with our armies" (verse 10), but expresses confidence that God will "tread down our foes" (verse 12).

In Psalm 79, we are given little evidence about the image of God and how the psalmist wants God to intervene, unless "flock of your pasture" can be considered a reference to God as shepherd (verse 13). In other respects, however, the narrative pattern of the community lament is present. The enemies are the nations (verse 1), they taunt Israel (verses 4, 12), the people are "brought very low" (verse 8), God is asked to avenge the people, and, then, they will "give thanks" forever (verse 13).

In Psalm 80, God is addressed as "Shepherd of Israel" (verse 1) and "Lord God of Hosts" (verse 7). The first is a common metaphor for a king in the ancient Near East and the second refers to God as leading a military host. A national defeat, remembered in metaphorical language of a garden ravaged by wild animals, forms the centerpiece of the psalm. There is little indication of how the psalmist expects God to intervene, aside from the repeated petition that God's "face shine" on them (verses 3, 7, 19). Praise is anticipated (verse 18).

Among psalms that some scholars might not, but some would, include in the community laments, four have elements of the narrative pattern. Psalm 58 begins in the council of the Gods ("Do you indeed decree what is right, you gods?" [verse 1]). The psalmist's petition envisions a fight or battle, for the righteous "will bathe their feet in the blood of the wicked" (58:10). The psalm ends with the righteous rejoicing (verse 10) and God being confirmed as judge of Earth (verse 11). Although a storm theophany, or a battle against chaos, are not mentioned, the image of God as warrior and judge and the narrative pattern—from divine council to battle on Earth—followed by rejoicing, is the same.

In Psalm 85, a march appears to be in view when the final verse says righteousness "will make a path for [God's] steps" (verse 13). In a beautiful passage, Earth responds to the divine march with justice (verses 10–11) and fertility (verse 12). This psalm is unique in that it expresses less complaint and more confidence than many other laments. As a result, the focus is on the latter part of the pattern.

Psalm 108 assumes God is a divine warrior and has the typical narrative pattern. The psalmist remembers God's promises made "in his sanctuary" (verse 7). The picture of Ephraim as God's helmet, Judah as God's scepter with God saying "over Philistia I shout in triumph" assumes an image of God as king and warrior (verse 9). The psalmist then laments that "you do not go out, O God, with our armies" (verse 11) and expresses confidence that God "will tread down our foes" (verse 13 par. 60:12). The imagery is clearly of God as warrior and assumes a narrative pattern where God as warrior will go forth from the sanctuary and defeat Israel's enemies.

Psalm 123 is brief, but addresses God as "enthroned in the heavens" (verse 1), which may refer to God as leader of the divine council, and mentions that they are victims of the scorn and contempt of the proud and lazy (verse 3–4). Although Psalm 123 is only four verses, these verses contain two elements of the typical narrative pattern.

By way of summary thus far, explicit imagery of the divine warrior myth is present in five community laments (Pss 74, 83, 89, 106, 144). These also contain elements of the narrative pattern. While the imagery may not be as explicit, eight other psalms seem to assume the imagery of God as warrior and have elements of the narrative pattern (Pss 44, 58, 60, 79, 80, 85, 108, 123). That means that out of a total of eighteen community laments, thirteen have elements of the divine warrior pattern. Five have explicit imagery and the narrative pattern, eight assume the imagery and have elements of the narrative pattern.

Among the remaining psalms (Pss 12, 90, 126, 129, 137), only Psalms 90 and 137 are widely recognized as community laments. Psalm 90 probably refers to conceptions of creation different than the battle of the divine warrior: "Before the mountains were brought forth, or ever you had formed the earth and the world" (verse 2). The allusion is probably not to creation by battle, but creation by birthing. As in the typical pattern, however, there is then a movement toward a response of praise (verse 14).

Among community laments, Psalm 137 has several anomalous elements and few of the regular form and content indicators of a community lament. Verses 5–6 are a vow. It could be argued that the "waters" are a reference to the sea in the mythological pattern or that mythologically "Babylon" is equivalent to the waters of chaos, so "rivers of Babylon" (verse 1) represent the chaos against which the divine warrior fights. In terms of the typical narrative, they are taunted by their enemies, in this case tormented by their captors (verse 3). Their inability to sing and vow not to forget Jerusalem may anticipate a day when they will be able to sing in Jerusalem (verses 4–6). So even these community laments may assume the imagery and pattern. In any case, the imagery and narrative pattern is widely enough attested to consider it typical of the genre of community lament.

In summary, the community lament has a typical cast of characters, imagery, and implied plot. God, the enemies, and the psalmist are the typical characters as in the individual lament. The enemies have similar characteristics to those in the individual laments; they taunt the people and plot against them, but now they are national enemies. The memory of past acts of God creates tension with current realities and the expectation that God will intervene in the future to establish justice. The divine warrior myth has influenced the narrative, and God is often portrayed as king, warrior, and judge intervening to defeat the mythological and historical enemies of the people. The imagery of the battle against the Sea is frequent, in contrast to the individual lament where the imagery of the battle against Death was more common and, as the next three chapters will show, with hymns where God as warrior and a battle are in the background or absent altogether.

Moby Dick and Free Willy

Hermann Melville's classic American novel *Moby Dick* and the remarkably successful series of *Free Willy* movies are examples of the use of this mythic pattern for social symbolic reflection on humanity's place in nature.[11] It was Northrop Frye who argued that classical and biblical myths provided the major sources of imagery for western literature, at least until the eighteenth century and perhaps beyond. He identified *Moby Dick* as a secular version of biblical myth.[12] Whereas *Moby Dick*'s use of the pattern relies directly on the Bible, *Free Willy*'s use of the pattern probably comes through *Moby Dick* and other cultural sources. As will become evident, the two whales represent very different reflections on society and ecology.

The story of *Moby Dick* is well known. Captain Ahab, who has lost his leg in a previous encounter with Moby Dick, leads a whaling expedition from Nantucket to the Indian and Pacific Oceans in search of revenge. The novel is clearly intended to be understood symbolically, because the narrator often comments on the symbolic, philosophical, existential, and spiritual meaning of realities like the sea. The novel makes extensive references and allusions to the Bible.

The novel's imagery and plot have many similarities to the biblical pattern. Whales in general and Moby Dick in particular are often called *Leviathans*. The author portrays Moby Dick as a mythic, almost divine figure. The role of the god in the narrative is played by Captain Ahab. Ahab goes *down* to the sea to do battle with Leviathan.

Ahab is named after an Israelite king who "did evil in the sight of the LORD more than all who were before him" (1 Kgs 16:30). Although human, Ahab's quest has a spiritual overlay that includes a desire for divine knowledge that will come from the depths. The wisdom that is present in the seas is evident when the African American cabin boy, Pip, almost drowns:

> By the merest chance the ship itself at last rescued him; but from that hour the little negro went about the deck an idiot; such, at least, they said he was. The sea had jeeringly kept his finite body up, but drowned the infinite of his soul. Not drowned entirely, though. Rather carried down alive to wondrous depths, where strange shapes of the unwarped primal world glided to and fro before his passive eyes; and the miser-merman, Wisdom, revealed his hoarded heaps; and among the joyous, heartless, ever-juvenile eternities, Pip saw the multitudinous, God-omnipresent, coral insects, that out of the firmament of waters heaved the colossal orbs. He saw God's foot upon the treadle of the loom, and spoke it; and therefore his shipmates called him mad. So man's insanity is heaven's sense; and wandering from all mortal reason, man comes at last to that celestial thought, which, to reason, is absurd and frantic; and weal or woe, feels then uncompromised, indifferent as his God.[13]

Ahab dies, but the narrator, Ishmael, survives to relate the glories of the battle and the knowledge gained by encounter with Leviathan. Thus, the novel is a secular version of the divine warrior myth.

In the novel, the mythic pattern is a symbolic reflection on society and ecology. On one level, the book is about American identity. The Pequod is symbolic of the United States of America. The crew is a veritable United Nations, with representatives of the poor of the

United States and many other nations. The narrator Ishmael is from an inland area of the United States, which, in his recounting, provided many excellent whalers. The first fellow whaler he meets in the novel, Queequeg, is Maori from New Zealand. The book praises the prowess of American whalers, especially those from Nantucket. Their prowess is compared to the whaling fleets of other nations, key representatives of whom they meet on the high seas—the French and the British. The Pequod, therefore, symbolizes a nation of farmers and immigrants. The descriptions of American contributions to the technology of whaling are just one example of American ingenuity and technical innovation, which makes them leaders in the exploitation of Earth's resources.

In addition, the name of the ship, the Pequod, recalls the colonial history of the United States. Melville briefly alludes to the origin of the name: "Pequod, you will no doubt remember, was the name of a celebrated tribe of Massachusetts Indians, now extinct as the ancient Medes."[14] The Pequod, sometimes also spelled Pequot, were a Connecticut tribe that was largely exterminated in wars with New England settlers. The immediate cause of the last Pequot war was the killing of a trader by three Pequot Indians, but some historians think the fact that the Pequot fort was in a strategic location may also have influenced the settlers. In any case, the name of the ship is a remembrance of the colonial history of the country it represents.

Melville's *Moby Dick* and the movie *Free Willy* construct very different understandings of whales, and by symbolic extension nature. In *Moby Dick* the whale is explicitly identified as Leviathan, the monster of the deep. Moby Dick attacks and destroys the ship. The whale is clearly the enemy; the relationship to nature antagonistic. In the opening scene of the first *Free Willy* movie, the name of the ship that is trying to trap Willy is briefly visible through the nets being dropped over the stern—Pequod. The screenwriters obviously made a clear connection between their movie and *Moby Dick*, and many other allusions make this clear. Because Moby Dick and Willy are both whales, readers and viewers could make the connection, even if it were not intended, because both are part of the larger culture and, thus, what whale could mean as a symbol.

The contrast in the portrayal of the two whales is striking. Already in the first scene, the viewer is encouraged to identify with Willy. We watch from Willy's point of view as nets separate him from his pod and watch them swim slowly away, with the sound of plaintive calls and sorrowful music. In the first movie, a troubled young boy, Jessie, befriends the whale. When Jessie discovers that Willy's owners have tried to kill Willy to collect the insurance, he manages, with the help of others, to return Willy to the sea, his family, and freedom. The third movie in the *Free Willy* trilogy comes full circle when Willy and Jessie help stop illegal whalers.

In their article "From *Moby Dick* to *Free Willy*," Thomas B. Lawrence and Nelson Phillips trace the dramatic change in metacultural attitudes toward whales.[15] In Melville's time, whales were considered a limitless, common resource. Some decline in the resource may already be evident in *Moby Dick* because long, deep-ocean voyages were made necessary by the decline of whale stocks in coastal areas. Beginning in 1930, regulations began to be put in place to protect declining whale stocks. Initially the concerns and discourse were financial. The regulations in 1930 arose because overfishing had driven prices down. Later, as stock began to decline, regulations were implemented to conserve and protect the resource. With this decline in whale numbers, a scientific discourse developed about whales as a species with declining and endangered populations. This discourse eventually led to the 1982 moratorium on whaling, which virtually ended commercial whaling. In addition to this scientific language, in their efforts to end whaling, Greenpeace early began using ethical language about whales as sentient beings who were inherently worthy of respect. When scientific evidence began to show that whales could survive as species with the resumption of limited commercial whaling, other conservation organizations like the World Wildlife Fund began to use ethical, rather than scientific, language to argue against a resumption of whaling. In the meta-cultural discourse, whales had gone from a natural resource, to an endangered species, to beings inherently valuable and worthy of respect.[16]

Around the same time as the whaling moratorium came into effect in 1982, Hollywood movies shifted from negative to positive portrayals of whales. Until the 1980s, movies like *Moby Dick*, *Pinocchio*, and *Orca* portrayed the whale negatively. Beginning in the eighties, a series of positive portrayals of whales began to appear in Hollywood movies. These movies reflected and supported the changing perception of whales in the broader culture. The movie *Free Willy* is the epitome of this trend.[17]

The stated purpose of the narrator of *Moby Dick* is to glorify the profession of whale hunting. This implies that, even in the seventeen and eighteen hundreds, the profession had a poor reputation—this seems to have been because of the inherent dangers and hardships, the low class of many whalers, and the smell of dead whales that returning whaling ships brought into the harbor—not because of any feeling that it was unethical to hunt whales. In order to glorify whale hunting, the narrator extols the whale, sometimes with religious language comparing whales to divinity. In other places, whales are compared to human beings, as in a chapter that describes the peaceful scene of cows nursing calves. Thus whales are described both as like humans and like gods. Within the novel, the purpose seems to be to make the whale a worthy adversary for the hunter. Although the adversary is admired, no questions are raised about the ethics of hunting whales. The relationship with nature is clearly antagonistic.

The novel continues to be read as a classic, and, in a changed cultural climate, this praise of whales' human and divine features could contribute to a contemporary discourse about the similarities of whales to humans and their almost sacred status.

Although there are no direct allusions to *Moby Dick* that I recall, the movie *Whale Rider* is interesting in this respect.[18] A young Maori girl fights to fulfill her destiny, which her grandfather denies, but eventually gains recognition as the long awaited whaler rider. The movie reflects the changing status of women in society and perhaps the rediscovery of the relevance of indigenous Maori spirituality to express the sense of the whale and other creatures as sacred and related to humans. Thus the whale continues to be used in this movie in symbolic reflection on society and ecology.

Moby Dick and *Free Willy* symbolize the changing relationship of humanity to nature. The *Free Willy* series reverses the order, running back through *Moby Dick* to the Bible, and imagines a different relationship to nature. The Leviathan of Job and *Moby Dick*, the whale of Jonah and *Pinocchio*, is now a beloved friend. Another *Moby Dick* movie was made in 1998, so the antagonistic relationship to nature persists in society alongside the more friendly relationship. Moreover, recognizing large mammals as inherently valuable because of their similarities to humans is not yet a recognition of all species as inherently valuable, but it is still a major cultural shift. Because the primary concern of this work and my area of expertise in the Hebrew Bible, this discussion of contemporary forms of the mythic pattern has necessarily been rather brief and superficial, but I hope it is sufficient to indicate the way this narrative pattern and associated imagery continues to function in contemporary society as symbolic reflection that constructs ecological reality.

These two chapters have shown that individual and communal laments have an implied narrative and recurring imagery that contribute to the construction of the faith world of the first three books of the Psalter. Both individual and communal laments share some of the same narrative patterns and images, and each has distinctive elements. The cry of the psalmist comes to God who sits as king in the divine council. The enemies of the psalmist are often described as wild animals. In the individual lament, they exhibit false friendliness, deceptive speech, and conspire to entrap or kill the psalmist. In community laments, their actions are usually in the past, rather than planned in the future, and they taunt and deride the community for their misfortunes. The contrast between past acts of God and current suffering creates tension, and petitions and praise anticipates a resolution in the future. God hears the cry of the psalmist and comes forth in a thunderstorm to do battle against the historical and mythic enemies of the psalmist. Individual laments have imagery similar to Baal's battle against Death. God delivers the psalmist from sinking into Sheol, the Pit, or the waters, puts them on a rock, and brings them to the temple and mountain of God. Communal laments have imagery similar to Baal's battle against Sea. God comes forth to do battle against national enemies, Sea, and sea monsters like Leviathan and Rahab. The psalmist celebrates a time when community is restored, God is worshipped in the temple on Mount Zion, and Earth community responds with joy, praise, and fertility.

Because laments are the dominant genre in the first three books, they create the faith world of these books. As laments, they express the reality of those in the depths of suffering, despair, and alienation. The fourth and fifth books continue to have laments and the narrative patterns and images of laments, but praise in the form of thanksgiving and hymns become more frequent. The structure of laments and the structure of the Psalter moves toward hymns, so the following chapters focus on hymns. They will show that hymns

have a different implied narrative and imagery, and a different understanding of God, humanity, and ecology.

CHAPTER 4

"The LORD, Maker of Heaven and Earth"

CREATION AND ITS IMPORTANCE

B iblical scholars have shown an increasing interest in creation theologies in the last few decades, often in the hope that creation theologies might help church and society address the global ecological crisis. Most recent studies of creation, however, have focused on only a few psalms (Pss 8, 104) and seldom appreciated the extent and contribution of creation to the final shape of the Psalter. This chapter is the first of several chapters that focus on hymns in the Psalter. Because the movement within genres and within the final form of the Psalter is toward praise, this examination of hymns is simultaneously a description of the conclusion to the shape and message of the Psalter. This chapter will show that hymns and creation play a key role in the canonical shape and message of the Psalter.

Definition of Creation

To begin, it is important to define what I mean by "creation" because the word can be used to refer to many different things. It may be used at one end of the spectrum quite narrowly to refer to original creation of the world out of nothing or at the other end of the spectrum quite broadly, almost as a synonym for nature, referring to all things created. Biblical scholars have had a number of debates about how to define the word. Some have argued that creation should only refer to the original creation of the world, but others have argued that the biblical concept of creation includes ongoing creation.

One of the issues in this debate has been whether the mythic pattern of the approach of God in a storm should be called a creation myth. Arvid Kapelrud argues that the battle of Baal against Sea and related biblical texts are not *creation* because "creation is when something new which was not there before is produced."[1] Dennis McCarthy insists that "the word *creation* in its normal context must mean some sort of absolute beginning of the world or we equivocate."[2]

These authors, however, are imposing a theological definition on the English word and on the biblical and ancient Near Eastern evidence. In English, when humans create, it refers to the creation of something new but not necessarily creation out of nothing or an absolutely new beginning. Similarly, John Gray argues, in the ancient Near East, Baal's battles against Sea can be considered creation in their ancient Near Eastern cultural context. He points out that "initial creation was not sharply distinguished by the ancient Mesopotamians from the regular sustaining of ordered nature."[3] For example, the Mesopotamian myth *Enuma Elish* tells the story of Marduk defeating Tiamat and creating sky and Earth out of Tiamat's body, but the account begins with a story of the birth of pairs of gods who, like

Tiamat (Salt Water) and her lover Apsu (Fresh Water), were embodiments or personifications of elements of the world. Matter was already present when Marduk created sky and Earth. The myths of Baal are creation myths in the sense that Baal's victory and reign brings order to the cosmos and makes life possible. When Baal dies in the myth of Baal and Death, then there is drought, crop failure, and death.[4] When Baal's sister Anat defeats Death and brings Baal up from the underworld, rain and fertility resume.[5] Similarly, when Baal defeats Sea and becomes king of the gods, Earth responds with the fertility necessary for life to flourish. R. J. Clifford says that in the Baal myths and related texts in the Bible, the "new thing" is "not primarily the physical universe as such, but the 'world' of men and women."[6] The Baal epic is a cosmogony in the sense that Baal creates the cosmos of rain and drought, feast and famine, and life and death in which humans live.[7]

Even the well-known story of creation in Genesis 1 may not speak of an absolute beginning or creation out of nothing. The Hebrew of the first verse can be translated "in the beginning of God's creating" or "when God began creating," so the stuff of creation is already present, and the story is about God's creation of order. Ben Ollenburger observes that limiting creation to "absolute beginning" makes it "almost impossible" to talk about creation in the Bible because there are so few passages. He argues that the witness of the Bible should determine what we mean by creation.[8] In my opinion, the definition of creation as original creation out of nothing (*ex nihilo*) is a later Christian, theological interpretation, which may contain important wisdom but would limit our appreciation of the biblical evidence.

The Hebrew word *bara'*, "create," which is used as a technical term for God's creative activity in Genesis 1, is used elsewhere for God's ongoing creation. For instance, the book of Isaiah uses the word to refer to both original and ongoing creation: "I form light and create darkness, make peace and create evil" (45:7; author translation). The word is used of ongoing creation in Isa 41:20 where it refers to God's renewal of the wilderness and in Isa 48:7 where it refers to things that were only recently created. Similarly, Psalms uses the word of generations that are "still to be created" (102:19). Psalm 104, the lengthy creation psalm, uses the word for ongoing creation: "When you send forth your spirit, they are created; and you renew the face of the ground" (verse 30). Clearly *bara'* includes both God's original and ongoing creation.

Related to the question of whether God's creative activity in the Bible includes ongoing creation is the question of whether blessing and fertility are part of God's creative activity. Claus Westermann wants to limit creation to original creation and speak of God's ongoing, providential care for the world as *blessing*.[9] Westermann wrote in a period when it was common for biblical scholars to say that Israel's God was a God of history and not of nature. He was actually arguing against an exclusive focus on God's historical deliverance and a recovery of blessing as God's ongoing, providential care. But evidently he did not want to go so far as to recognize blessing as ongoing creation. Westermann's desire to separate creation and blessing may be a reflection of reading the evidence through the lens of western culture's dichotomy between God and nature.

The Psalms, however, clearly and repeatedly relate God's work as Creator with blessing and fertility. (The biblical concept of blessing has fertility at its core.[10]) The mythic pattern of the "storm god" has the outpouring of fertility as part of the pattern, and this pattern continues in the Psalms. There is a natural connection between storm imagery for God and the rains that bring life and fertility to a dry land. Thus, the outpouring of fertility is a recurring part of the mythic pattern of the storm god in the ancient Near East and Israel. The Psalms regularly connect God's work as Creator with blessing and fertility (65:9-13; 144:12-15). Psalm 104 begins with a section that uses storm imagery for God as Creator (verses 2–9), which then flows into a lengthy description of God's presence in creation providing fertility and blessing (verses 10–30). Both the juxtaposition of creation and fertility and the verbal connections make it clear that it is the Creator who creates fertility and blessing in support of the life of all creatures. Even texts that do not use storm imagery or the verb *bara'* link the Creator with blessing: "May you be blessed by the LORD, who makes skies and Earth" (Ps 115:15; author translation; see, by way of comparison, also Gen 14:19; Pss 121:2; 124:8; 134:3; 146:5-6). God's work as Creator, therefore, includes God's presence in the world providing the fertility necessary for diverse and abundant life.

Biblical scholars have also debated the relationship between creation and salvation. My own sense is that God as Creator and savior are more closely related than many have imagined, but remain distinct because the imagery of God as Creator is related to certain types of salvation. It is not necessary to enter into the debate on the relation between creation and salvation here, which has been discussed at length by Terence Fretheim,[11] except to note the discussion that follows will make a case for the relationship between creation and liberation.

This debate may overlook an aspect of the classical creation stories in Genesis 1–3 and the Psalter that is more important for the present study. The articles in *Cosmogony and Ethical Order* document the way that cosmogonies, stories of the origin of the world, are related to ethics in a wide variety of cultures and religions. According to the editors, Robin W. Lovin and Frank E. Reynolds, cosmogonic myths "are attempts to find a pattern of human choice and action that stands outside the flux of change and yet within the bounds of human knowing."[12] The contributors to their volume show that, in a wide variety of cultures and religions, cosmogonies reflect "a tradition's most general ideas about reality."[13] William Brown points out that "biblical scholarship has . . . almost entirely forgotten that at the heart of creation's mythos is a moral ethos."[14] While agreeing with Brown that the relation of *mythos* to *ethos* has been overlooked in biblical studies, I define *mythos* and *ethos* a little differently than he does. I define *mythos* as the typical imagery and implied narrative of a genre and *ethos* as the social, political, and ecological worlds that *mythos* creates, or could create. This chapter is particularly interested in the *mythos* of the hymn as a genre and what kinds of social, political, and ecological *ethos* that *mythos* imagines or could be used to imagine.

Ronald Simkins, William Brown, and Terence Fretheim, in separate studies, have all listed the wide variety of creation images and language that are used in the Hebrew Bible.[15] Several clusters of imagery and vocabulary will occur particularly frequently in the following discussion because they are recurring images with stereotypical language. By way of preview, God's approach in a storm, which we have already seen in lament and thanksgiving, recurs in hymns. Frank Moore Cross has distinguished between two types of the march of God in a storm,[16] and it is the second type, where battle has receded in the background or disappeared entirely, that is most common in hymns. The words "establishing" (*kwn*) and "founding" (*ysd*) Earth are common with this imagery. The language of God "making" (*'sh*) and "forming" (*ytsr*) is common with human creation. Towards the end of the Psalter, the language of God "making" (*'sh*) occurs frequently with creation of the world or parts of the world and seems to presuppose an image of God as builder or architect.

Some pitch the tent of "creation" so broadly that it would include any reference to nature in the Psalms. Such a definition is so broad as to be almost meaningless for the present work of defining recurring imagery and story lines in genres. But this raises the question of whether nature's praise of God is related to the story of God's creative activity in the Psalms. I would include it in the discussion of creation because psalms often place it alongside other creation motifs and sometimes express a relationship. For example, the connection between Creator and creatures' praise of the Creator is made explicit when Psalm 145 says:

> The LORD is good to all,
>> and his compassion is over all his works (*ma'asav*).
> All your works (*ma'asekha*) shall give thanks to you, O LORD,
>> and all your faithful shall bless you. (verses 9–10; author translation)

The same Hebrew word here translated "works" is used in both verses. It has a wide range of meanings that can include things created by humans or God. The works give thanks to the God who created and, in the biblical understanding, continues to create them. God's creation of all creatures is the reason they praise the Creator. Therefore, the understanding of creation in Psalms includes creation's praise of the Creator.

In summary, the biblical understanding of creation is not limited to original creation out of nothing but includes any account of the origin of the cosmos. This includes both original and ongoing creation, blessing, fertility, and the sustaining of abundant life. Especially important for this study are the typical imagery and implied narrative of creation and the way they might be used in the construction of ancient and contemporary social, political, and ecological realities. By way of preview, the recurring imagery for creation in hymns is the approach of God in a storm, the making of the world as a builder or architect, the resulting life and fertility, and creation's response with joy and praise of the Creator.

The Shape of the Psalter

Hymns play an important role in the final form of the Psalter. Laments predominate in the early books of the Psalter, and thanksgiving and hymns come to predominate in the later books so that there is a movement through the Psalter from lament to praise. Only a few creation hymns appear in the first three books, but groups of hymns that speak of creation appear at key locations in the last two books. In the first three books, Psalms 8, 19, 29, 33, 47 are among the few hymns that speak of creation and the Creator. In book four, there is a group of what are often called enthronement hymns, or hymns to God as king (Psalms 93, 95–99), that are centrally located and central to the message of the book. These names for the genre focus on the image of king, but, as we will see, these psalms speak frequently and at length about creation and the Creator. Psalm 100 also speaks of creation. Then Psalm 104, which is one of the longest creation texts in the Bible, is part of a series of psalms that have been placed as a conclusion to the fourth book and segue to the fifth.

In the fifth book, creation appears frequently and at key locations in hymns and related genres. A hymnic phrase unique to this book appears in a number of genres and collections. The NRSV translates the phrase as either "the LORD, who made heaven and earth" (Pss 115:15; 121:2; 124:8; 146:6), or "the LORD, maker of heaven and earth" (134:3). Psalm 136 has a phrase that may be related because it has the same verb and structure: "the LORD . . . who made the great lights" (136:1-7). This translation of the verb as "made" or "maker" may reflect an assumption that creation is original creation. In all these cases, the Hebrew could be translated "the LORD, who *makes*." So these recurring phrases may refer to ongoing creation. The Hebrew participial form translated "makes" is one of the formal characteristics of the genre of hymns and indicates the origin of this phrase in hymns. In addition, creation hymns appear at the seam between two collections (Psalms 135, 136) and, most significantly, in a group of psalms that form the conclusion to the Psalter (Psalms 145–150).

Some time ago now, Westermann noticed that there is a movement within the genres from lament to praise.[17] Most laments have confessions of trust or vows to praise that may include hymnic elements. These laments are remembered in thanksgiving, which will also include praise of God. The general praise of God may appear in thanksgiving, where God is praised for specific acts, but this general praise of the character of God is characteristic of hymns. Thus, within genres and between genres, there is a movement from lament to praise of God.

This movement in the genres from lament to praise is reproduced in the shape of the Psalter as a book. More laments appear in the early books and more praise (thanksgiving psalms and hymns) in the later books.[18] Scholars vary somewhat on which psalms they would designate laments, but, by my count, laments are twenty-seven of the forty-one psalms in the first book, nineteen of the thirty-one psalms in the second book, ten of the twenty-seven psalms in the third book, four of the seventeen psalms in the fourth book, and thirteen of the thirty-four psalms in the fifth book. Or, the percentage of lament psalms decreases from 61 percent in the first book and 62 percent in the second book, to 48 percent in the third book, 24 percent in the fourth book, and 38 percent in the fifth book.

Similarly, scholars vary somewhat on which psalms they designate as hymns, but there is general agreement that the number and frequency of hymns increases through the Psalter. Nancy deClaissé-Walford says hymns make up eight of forty-one psalms, or 20 percent of book one, six out of thirty-one psalms, or 19 percent of book two, six out of seventeen psalms, or 35 percent of book three, five out of seventeen psalms, or 24 percent of book four, and twenty-three of forty-four psalms, or 52 percent of book five.[19] Her classification of "hymns" is a little different than mine. She calls thanksgiving psalms "hymns of thanksgiving" and includes them in her count of "hymns." Thus her classification system recognizes the relationship between "thanksgiving" and "hymn" as does Westermann's classification of both as "praise."[20] I used what I perceive to be the more widely used designations "thanksgiving" for psalms that give thanks to God for something, and "hymn" for psalms that are more general praise of the character of God. Nevertheless, deClaissé-Walford's way of counting psalms does bring out the movement within the Psalter, because thanksgiving psalms usually move towards and include some general, hymnic description of God's character. In addition to thanksgiving psalms, other genres contain hymnic material and hymns appear at key locations in the final books, including the five hymns that form a conclusion to the Psalter (Psalms 145–150). Therefore, the genres move from lament to hymns, and this is reproduced on a larger scale in the Psalter, which shifts from more lament in the early books to more thanksgiving and hymns in the later books.

For this reason, both hymns and creation tend to be infrequent in the first three books of the Psalter (Psalms 1–41, 42–72, 73–89). When creation does occur, it is usually the march of the divine warrior that we have seen in laments, because laments are frequent in these books. As will become evident after these psalms have been discussed in more detail, different types of references to creation and the imagery for God as Creator appear in hymns, especially towards the end of the Psalter, and this creates a shift in the understanding of creation as a reader journeys through the Psalter.

God as Ruler and Creator

The fourth book of the Psalter (Psalms 90–106) tells the story of the exile.[21] The third book ends with a psalm that mourns the broken covenant with David (Psalm 89). The fourth book begins with the only psalm with the superscription, "A Prayer of Moses" (Psalm 90:1), as if to remind the people of an earlier model of leadership. The grand experiment of kingship had failed miserably. In the telling of the Deuteronomistic history, there had been only a few good kings, and these were not enough to compensate for the sins of the others. Many people had been sent into exile. The pillars of their faith and culture—temple, land, and king—had been destroyed or removed. It is evident both in the book of Psalms and many other writings that can be dated to this period that particularly important in rebuilding the faith was an understanding of God as Creator. The story of creation that introduces the Bible (Genesis 1) is usually dated to this period. And God is frequently described as Creator in the exilic part of the book of Isaiah. Thus the fourth book in the Psalms corresponds to the exile when God as Creator gained new prominence.

Many scholars agree with Gerald Wilson that the enthronement psalms are the "theological 'heart'" both of the fourth book and of the entire Psalter.[22] In what follows, I will suggest that creation plays such a prominent role in these psalms that one could say that creation lies at the theological heart of the Psalter.

In the midst of the fourth book, there is a significant cluster of enthronement hymns (Psalms 93, 95–99) that speak of creation. Prominent in the enthronement hymns is the exclamation "the LORD reigns" (Pss 93:1; 96:10; 97:1; 99:1; author translation) or "God reigns" (Ps 47:8; author translation). Most scholars would also include Psalm 98 among the enthronement psalms because it uses similar language to call for the praise of "the King, the LORD" (verse 6). The name *enthronement psalms* comes from speculation by some biblical scholars, based on practices in neighboring cultures, that these hymns were used in an annual ritual that reenacted God's defeat of the powers of chaos, the establishment of order, and enthronement of God as king. We know that such a ceremony was celebrated annually in Babylon. In the Babylonian myth *Enuma Elish*, "When on High," the god Marduk defeats the god Tiamat, constructs the skies and the land out of her body, and becomes king of the gods.[23] This is, of course, a Mesopotamian example of the widespread ancient Near Eastern mythic pattern that we saw in laments. On a political level, this myth explains why the city of Babylon, whose god was Marduk, came to rule over other Mesopotamian cities. The yearly reenactment of this myth with the king of Babylon playing the role of Marduk would legitimate the status of the king and Babylon.[24] While there is little or no evidence that such a ceremony was celebrated in Israel, these enthronement hymns have much of the same imagery of defeat of the waters of chaos and enthronement of God as king.

These enthronement psalms frequently refer to God as Creator. Psalm 93 praises God who "has established the world" (verse 1). Psalm 95 says, "The sea is his, for he made it, and the dry land, which his hands have formed" (verse 5) and calls the people to worship "the LORD, our Maker" (verse 6). Psalm 96 says that "God made the skies" (verse 5; author translation) and because of God "the world is firmly established" (verse 10). Psalm 100, which is not an enthronement hymn but comes immediately after them, calls for worship of God who "made us" (verse 3). The theme of creation's praise of the Creator runs through these psalms and foreshadows the reappearance of this motif in several psalms that conclude the Psalter. Calls to sing or "make a joyful noise" to God all Earth (Pss 96:1, 9; 98:4; 100:1) and even more elaborate calls for various parts of creation to praise God appear in several psalms (96:11-13; 98:7-8) and anticipate similar calls in the psalms that conclude the Psalter (Psalms 145–150). In fact, creation is so prominent in these psalms that it could be said that they celebrate God as ruler and Creator. Creation, therefore, appears prominently in these psalms that are central to the message of the fourth book.

The message of these psalms is particularly relevant to the exile. The people have experienced the abject failure of the monarchy to provide faithful leadership and no longer have a king. These psalms assert that they do not need a human king because God is their king. The temple has been destroyed and they have been removed from the land, but the enthronement psalms picture all creation as a place of worship and all creation as their land. Thus, the loss of king, temple, and land is answered by the message of God as ruler and Creator.

Creation is also prominent in the conclusion to the fourth book. Psalm 104 is one of the longest accounts of creation in the Bible and is integrated into a series of psalms (Psalms 103–106) that conclude the fourth book of the Psalter. In recent years, biblical scholars have noticed some of the links between these Psalms, but because this information is new and not much has been said about the role creation plays, I will discuss the links and the role of creation at some length. Taken together, they form a conclusion to this book that is a theological summary of exilic, creation theology.

Among the indications that these psalms are designed to be read together are a number of repeated words and phrases. Psalm 103 and Psalm 104 both begin and end with the same phrase, which is unique in the Bible to these two psalms—"Bless the Lord, O my soul."[25] Psalm 103 praises God "who *satisfies* you with *good*" (verse 5; author emphasis), and the same verb occurs three times in Psalm 104 to describe God who "satisfies" Earth (verse 13) and trees (verse 16) with water, and all creatures with food and with "good" (verse 28). The words in italics above and below represent repeated Hebrew words. These verbal relationships are indicative of the relationship between the content of these two psalms. The first psalm is about the relationship of the individual and worshipping community to God "who satisfies you with *good*" (Ps 103:5; author emphasis), and the second is about the relationship of the Creator with all creatures who are "filled with *good* things" (Ps 104:28; author emphasis).

The Hebrew word *ma'aseh*, "work," appears repeatedly in various forms. Psalm 103 ends with a call for all God's "works" to bless God (verse 22), and Psalm 104 then describes in some detail God's "works," ending with praise of the multitude of God's "works" (verse 24) and a prayer that God might rejoice in those "works" (verse 31). Psalm 106 expresses sorrow that Israel forgot God's "works" (verse 13) and instead followed the "works" of the nations (verse 35; author translation) and committed unclean "works" (verse 39; author translation).[26] Therefore, *works* run like a thread through these psalms, tying them together.

Psalms 104 and 105 are linked together by an almost identical string of verbs for praise appearing at the end of Psalm 104 and the beginning of Psalm 105. Towards the end of Psalm 104, the psalmist indicates an intention to pray and praise with a string of words: *shyr* "sing," *zmr* "praise," *sykh* "meditation," *smkh* "rejoice" (verses 33–34). A similar string of verbs occurs in Ps 105:2-3: *shyr* "sing," *zmr* "praise," *shykh* "meditate," *hll* "boast," *smkh* "rejoice." The differences are that in the first series, meditation appears as a noun with another verb rather than as a verb, and, in the second series, another verb, "boast," is inserted. Despite these minor differences, Patrick Miller argues that this series is unique in the Hebrew Bible and, therefore, links the two psalms.[27]

Another verbal connection is the word *wonderful*. Psalm 105 begins with calls to tell and remember God's "wonderful works" (verses 2, 5). These wonderful works for Israel are then described in Psalm 105. *Works* appear again in Psalm 106, but here Israel "did not consider your wonderful works" (verse 7), and forgot God's "wonderful works" (verse 22; author translation). Psalms 105 and 106 portray two different responses to God's wonders, but the word *wonders* ties the two psalms together.

Another word that creates connections between Psalm 104 and the psalms that follow is *hallelujah* (translated "Praise the LORD" in the NRSV). It is the last word of Psalm 104, the last word of Psalm 105, and the first and last word of Psalm 106. In fact, this word creates interesting connections between the concluding psalms of the fourth book and the psalms in the fifth book. The word *hallelujah* appears first as the last word of Psalm 104. In addition to the appearances in Psalms 105 and 106 just mentioned, it then appears on the beginning and end of a whole series of psalms in the fifth book.[28] The appearance of *hallelujah* at the beginning and ending of psalms that conclude the fourth book tie these psalms together and segues to psalms in the fifth book.

These fairly obvious repetitions of words and phrases are not the only connections an astute reader will make. Repeated vocabulary is only the most obvious manifestation of themes and imagery that create intertextual relationships. As was just mentioned, Psalm 105 calls the reader to tell and remember God's "wonderful works" (verses 2, 5). The NRSV makes explicit an association that is only implicit in the original text. The Hebrew word translated "wonderful works," often just translated "wonders" in English, is not related to the Hebrew word translated "works" in Psalm 104. Nevertheless, when Psalm 105 begins with these references to "wonders" and says "God's judgments are in all Earth" (verse 7; author translation), a reader may think of God's works in creation just praised extensively in Psalm 104. The choice of words distinguishes the types of works, but also connects them. This is just one indication that it is the Creator praised in Psalm 104 who does wonders in Psalm 105. The word used for "works" in Psalm 104 reappears in Psalm 106 indicating the relationship between the works and wonders in all these psalms. The "wonderful works" in Psalm 105 look backward to God's works in creation in Psalm 104 and forward to God's works in Israel in the rest of Psalm 105 and Psalm 106. It is the Creator of skies and Earth who is present and active in the life of Israel.

Psalm 103 and Psalm 104 share a similar narrative pattern and imagery for the Creator, though it is less explicit in Psalm 103. Allusions to the imagery and narrative pattern that we saw in lament psalms is evident in the reference to God who "redeems your life from the Pit" (Ps 103:4) and in the statement that God has "established" (*kwn*) a throne in the heavens (103:19). The throne is clearly royal imagery for God, and the word "established" is typical of the march of God in a storm.[29] In addition to the establishment of a throne, the mention of angels, ministers, and hosts (103:19-21) conjures up an image of the divine court, which is present in the mythic pattern. The narrative movement in Psalm 103 from redemption of the psalmist to enthronement of God is the narrative pattern of the storm theophany. The absence of reference to a battle is significant, but the imagery and narrative pattern of this psalm come from the mythic pattern of the storm theophany.

In the midst of Psalm 103, there is also an allusion to the creation of humankind: "For he knows how we were made; he remembers that we are dust" (verse 14). The Creator, who redeems and establishes dominion in the heavens, will have compassion, because God knows how humans were made and, thus, how fragile and transient human life is.

The imagery and narrative pattern of the storm theophany are clearer in Psalm 104 where, as we have seen, God appears in a storm theophany with all the attendant phenomena—clouds, rain. Therefore, 103 and 104 are both creation psalms.

As with the canonical form of the Torah, creation forms an introduction and foundation for the story of Israel that follows. In Genesis,
the story of the creation of the world (1:1-2:4a) precedes the story of
human creation. Likewise, Psalms 103 and 104 preserve two perspectives on creation, but in the reverse order to Genesis. Individual
thanksgiving (Psalm 103) precedes community praise of the Creator
(Psalm 104). As Miller puts it, "The one who redeems and heals the
sufferer, whether one or many, is also the one who stretched out the
heavens and provides the continuities of the universe's existence.
This joining of creation and history, of the universal and the particular, in God's 'works' is then underscored as Psalm 104 leads on into
the 'national' hymns of Psalms 105 and 106."[30] One and the same
Creator delivers individuals and the nation (Psalm 103), all creatures
(Psalm 104), and is the God of steadfast love throughout Israel's history (Psalm 105) against whom Israel has rebelled and asks for for-
giveness and restoration to the land (Psalm 106).

In addition to the verbal links between these psalms, God acts
as creator in nature in Psalms 105 and 106. In Psalm 105, it is God
who works in nature to summon the famine (verse 16) that sends
the people to Egypt and makes them fruitful in Egypt (verse 24). As
Fretheim has pointed out in the book of Exodus, God acts in nature
to redeem Israel from Egypt.[31] The account of the so-called plagues
in Psalm 105 is a reversal of creation and perversion of the blessing
described in Genesis 1. The sending of darkness (verse 28) reverses
the first act in Genesis 1, which was the creation of light. In Genesis
1, Earth brings forth vegetation and creatures, and the innumerable
creatures of the sea, which are blessed by God and told to be fruitful
and multiply, and God calls it good. By contrast, in Psalm 105, the
seas are turned to blood, the fish die (verse 29), and frogs swarm over
the land (verse 30). Instead of swarming in the sea, they swarm over
the land, and the land swarms with flies and gnats (verse 31). Instead

of watering Earth, rain falls as hail that destroys crops (verses 32–33). What hail does not get, innumerable locusts finish off (verses 34–35). The abundance that should have supported blessing and fertility has becomes a perverted, destructive force. Although the image of God is horrifying, the death of the firstborn of Egypt is the culmination of God's working in nature to reverse creation and blessing (verse 36). As Fretheim has also noted in other contexts, God's care for the people in the wilderness is portrayed as the restoration of creation, or re-creation. The cloud and fire that accompanied God's appearance in Ps 104:3-4 now leads the people in the wilderness in Ps 105:39. Food and water are restored in abundance (verses 40–41).

God also works as Creator in nature in Psalm 106. Psalm 106 begins and ends with praise and a petition that God would bring the individual psalmist and the nation back from exile. In the middle is a long expression of trust that forms the basis for the hope that the petition will be answered. The fact that they had so often sinned, yet God had continued to hear their cry and had delivered them, is the basis for a prayer that God will bring them back from exile. The wonders (verse 7) and "works" (verse 13) that the people did not remember are God's works in nature as Creator. The verb used for God's "rebuke" is typical language of the storm theophany, as is the use of "deep" (verse 9) for the Red Sea. God's power as Creator is evident in the use of the waters to cover the Egyptians (verse 11). Later, in the wilderness, judgment comes through disease (verse 15) and plague (verse 29), and Earth swallows Datham and Abiram (verse 17).[32] The fire and flame,[33] which appear with God as God's "ministers" or servants in Ps 104:4, burn up the wicked in Ps 106:18.[34] Israel's history, therefore, is grounded in and a part of the larger story of creation. God's activity in and with Israel is part of God's action in and with creation.

In summary, the many verbal, thematic, and narrative links between Psalms 103, 104, 105, and 106 show that they are to be read together as a conclusion to the fourth book. Taken together they form an integrated statement of an exilic theology of God as Creator. The Creator whose steadfast love and compassion is experienced in the life of the individual in healing, salvation, and justice (Ps 103) is also the God who cares for all creatures (Ps 104). The same Creator has acted through nature in the exodus and wilderness wandering. After this extensive praise of God's wonders and works as Creator, they confess that Israel had forgotten the Creator, and pray for a return from exile.

Maker of Heaven and Earth

Even more so than in the fourth book, creation plays a key role in the organization and theology of the fifth and final book of the Psalter. This fifth book tells the story of the Restoration. Cyrus the king of Persia allowed the Israelites to return to Jerusalem in 538 B.C.E. They eventually managed to rebuild the walls of Jerusalem and a small temple, but they were ruled by Persia. The fourth book ends with a prayer for restoration to the land (Psalm 106), and the fifth book begins with thanksgiving for restoration to the land (Psalm 107).

Hymns with creation themes appear at key locations in the organizational structure of this section of the Psalms. The fifth book of the Psalter contains a number of collections of psalms, which may have existed independently before being placed in the fifth book. There are two groups of psalms with the superscription "of David." These are placed near the beginning and end of the collection (Psalms 108–110, 138–145). These Davidic collections are each followed by collections of hallelujah psalms, so called because they begin or end with the word *hallelujah* (Psalms 111–118, 146–150). Psalm 135 is also a hallelujah psalm. Between these two David and hallelujah collections, and thus at the center of the organization of the fifth book, is a collection of songs of ascent.

The organization of these collections and the psalms without superscriptions that has created editorial seams between the collections may perhaps best be illustrated in the following chart:

Psalm 107	No superscription
Psalms 108–110	Of David
Psalms 111–117	Hallelujah. No superscriptions.
Psalms 118–119	No superscription
Psalms 120–134	Songs of Ascent
Psalms 135–137	No superscriptions
Psalms 138–145	Of David
Psalms 146–50	Hallelujah. No superscriptions.

Wilson has shown that psalms without superscriptions appear at the seams of collections and show evidence of intentional placement by editors.[35] The order of the collections and the presence of psalms without superscriptions at the seams of collections are evidence of a purposeful arrangement.

In this fifth section, the frequency of hymns and creation increases significantly. The focus of this chapter is creation in hymns, but the fifth book also contains references to creation in other genres. Psalm 107 is the community thanksgiving that begins this collection. It gives thanks for the rescue of sailors at sea using the language, imagery, and narrative pattern of the battle against the sea (verses 23–32). In the same psalm, God works in nature providing food and water (verses 4–8), healing the sick (verses 17–22), and providing water, food, blessing, and fertility (verses 33–38, 41). In anticipation of the discussion of creation and liberation in the next chapter, it could also be noted that this psalm, which speaks of God as Creator, active in nature, also gives thanks to God for the release of prisoners (verses 10–16) and for bringing down oppressors and raising up the oppressed (verses 39–41). Psalm 119, the great torah psalm whose size and central location dominate the fifth book, mentions human creation—"your hands have made ('sh) and fashioned (kvn) me" (verse 73)—and world creation—"you have established (kvn) Earth" (verse 90; author translation)—which may reflect the wisdom assumption that God's instruction is grounded in creation.

Psalms 121 and 124 are significant because they are songs of ascent, which are centrally located in the structure of the fifth book and give thanks to God who "makes ('sh) skies[36] and Earth" (Pss 121:2; 124:8; author translation). Superscriptions identify Psalms 120–134 as "songs of ascent," and internal clues suggest they were used in pilgrimages up to the temple. Jews use them at *Sukkoth*, "Booths," the festival that celebrates God's care for the Israelites in the wilderness. Psalms 121 and 124, therefore, are thanksgiving psalms that are part of the centrally located psalms of ascent and give thanks for help from God who "makes skies and Earth."

Psalms 138 and 139 begin a collection of psalms of David. Psalm 138, an individual thanksgiving, and Psalm 139, an individual lament, both refer to human creation (Pss 138:8; 139:13, 15). Finally, Psalm 144, a royal lament, asks God to intervene with the imagery of a storm (verses 5–6). Hymns, therefore, are not alone in their references to the Creator, but are part of a trend in the fourth book toward more frequent references to God as Creator.

Hymns that speak of the Creator and creation appear at key locations in the fifth book. Psalms 114 and 115 appear at the center of the first group of hallelujah psalms (Psalms 111–117). With the exception of Psalm 114, the psalms in this collection all begin or end with the word *hallelujah*.[37] *Hallelujah* is translated in some English translations as "Praise the Lord!" because *hallelujah* is a combination of an imperative "Praise!" and a short form of the name of God. Psalms 113–118 are sometimes called the Egyptian hallel psalms because they have the title "hallelujah" in the Septuagint, the Greek translation of the Bible. The inclusion of both Psalms 114 and 115 in the genre of hymn is debatable. Psalm 114 seems to have a setting in worship and hymnic mood but has none of the imperative calls to worship characteristic of hymns and only one hymnic participle (verse 8a).[38] Erhard Gerstenberger thinks Psalm 115 is a hymn, and the elements from other genres reflect the external and internal struggles of the worshipping community.[39] Psalm 115 has hymnic elements and elements of other genres so that some classify it as a liturgy. Psalm 114 identifies the Red Sea, the Jordan, and the primordial waters of chaos that flee before the coming of the storm God. Psalm 115 prays, "May you be blessed by the LORD, who makes skies and Earth" (verse 15; author translation).

Psalms 135 and 136 are two of three psalms without superscriptions between the songs of ascent and the concluding collections of David and hallelujah psalms. Psalm 135 says God "makes the clouds rise at the end of the earth . . . makes lightnings for the rain and brings out the wind" (verse 7). Psalm 136 contains quite a lengthy section praising God as Creator:

> who alone does great wonders,
>> for his steadfast love endures forever;
> who by understanding made the heavens,
>> for his steadfast love endures forever;
> who spread out Earth[40] on the waters,
>> for his steadfast love endures forever;
> who made the great lights,
>> for his steadfast love endures forever;
> the sun to rule over the day,
>> for his steadfast love endures forever;
> the moon and stars to rule over the night,
>> for his steadfast love endures forever. (verses 4–9)

This section is followed by a section giving thanks to God for the exodus and guidance in the wilderness (verses 10–16). The psalm also praises God "who gives food to all flesh" (verse 25). Thus Psalms 135 and 136 both praise God as Creator present in creation.

These hymns contain a number of references to the exodus and wandering in the wilderness. These references would have had symbolic meaning in the exile or restoration. Psalm 114 views the crossing of the Red Sea and the crossing of the Jordan as one event and describes them using the imagery of the march of the storm God. Psalm 135 praises God for bringing the people out of Egypt and bringing them into the promised land. Those who had returned from exile gave thanks for being in the promised land (Psalm 135), but still looked forward to deliverance from foreign rule (Psalm 114).

These references to the exodus are, as I have noted before, references to the Creator and God's work in nature. Psalm 114 uses the imagery of the march of the storm God to describe the crossing of the Red Sea and the Jordan. Psalm 135 places praise of God as a storm God (verses 5–7) immediately before praise of God for the deliverance from Egypt and entry into the promised land (verses 8–12). Thus, creation precedes exodus, and God acts in the exodus as Creator, working in and through nature (verses 8–9). The next psalm expands this pattern of creation preceding exodus and the Creator working in the exodus from Egypt. Psalm 136 describes creation (verses 4–9) and then the deliverance from Egypt (verses 10–22).

Psalms 145–150 all include references to Creator and creation and form the climax and conclusion of the Psalter. Psalm 145 is the final David psalm. Psalms 146–150 are the final hallelujah collection. The first of these, Psalm 145, is the last of the psalms with the superscription "Of David." Psalm 145 says:

The LORD is good to all,

    and his compassion is over all his works (*ma'asav*).

All your works (*ma'asekha*) shall give thanks to you, O LORD,

    and all your faithful shall bless you. (verses 9–10; author

      translation)

The same Hebrew word translated as "works" is used in both verses nine and ten. All things created give thanks to the God who created them. The last line places in David's mouth the confession that, by blessing God, the faithful take part in the praise of the Creator by all created things.

Psalm 146 praises God "who makes skies and Earth, the sea and all that is in them" (verse 6; author translation). The use of the participle "makes" suggests that ongoing creation is in view. The fact that this line is immediately followed by "who keeps faith forever" (verse 6), suggests that the reliability of creation is due to the faithfulness of the Creator. The verses that precede and follow this verse confirm that the Creator's work in creation is in view because the preceding verse speaks of happiness or blessedness, and the following verses speak of the provision of food.

Psalm 147 speaks of the Creator as the one who orders the stars and gives them their names (verse 4), who provides the clouds and rain that provide for plants (verse 8), who thereby makes food for animals (verse 9), who blesses (verse 13), who provides wheat (verse 14), and who sends snow, frost, hail, wind, and water (verses 16–18). As in the preceding psalm, the imagery of the storm God seems to be in view, not as a warrior, but as a provider of blessing within creation. God's work of command to nature is placed alongside God's word to Jacob (verses 18–19). As in Psalm 19, God's instruction is present both in creation and scripture.

Psalm 148 calls all parts of creation to praise God. Among those called are sun, moon, stars (verse 3), hail, snow, frost, mountains, hills, trees, animals, and birds (verses 8–10). The reason they should praise God is introduced, as is typical in hymns, by the word "for." The reason is that God is their Creator. God "created (*br'*). . . established them forever and ever" (verses 5–6). Brueggemann thinks that the lack of concrete reference to liberation in this psalm is an indication that creation theology forgets the cry of the oppressed and supports the status quo. This overlooks the fact that Psalm 148 comes after Psalms 146 and 147, which integrate creation and justice, and comes before Psalm 149, which is very much concerned with justice.

Psalm 149 calls Israel to praise the Lord and be glad in their Maker (verse 2). The word for *Maker* is from the same root as the word "makes" in the expression "who makes skies and Earth" that has appeared a number of times in the fifth book. "Maker" is in parallel with "King" in the next line. That the two are in parallel indicates that in some sense they are identified as the discussion of *Enuma Elish* has suggested; both are related in the ancient Near Eastern ideology of the king. In earlier parts of the Psalter, *king* was often used as the primary metaphor for God, but now this has been supplemented and modified by a renewed emphasis on God as Creator.

Creation Characteristic of Hymns

As I hope the frequency of references to creation in the foregoing discussion has begun to suggest, certain types of creation are characteristic of hymns. Admittedly, not every hymn contains some form of creation imagery, but neither does every element of a genre occur in every individual occurrence of that genre. Certain, recurring creation motifs occur frequently enough to say they are part of the genre of hymn.

Most of the hymns in books one to three refer to creation. Although hymns appear infrequently in books one to three, most of them refer to God as Creator. Several refer to some aspect of the storm theophany. Psalm 29 portrays God's appearance in a storm (verses 3–9), and Psalm 68 refers to God as the one "who rides upon the clouds" (verse 3), who showered "rain in abundance" (verse 9), and is the "rider in the skies" (verse 33). Psalm 8:3 says God "established" the moon and stars, and this language of "establishing" comes from the tradition of the storm theophany. The language of God "making" is used both of the skies (Ps 33:6) and humans (Ps 8:5). Also God "fashions the hearts" of humans in Ps 33:15. Among hymns in the first three books, only Psalm 47, an enthronement hymn, does not mention creation. Psalm 47, however, may be the exception that proves the rule, because creation is characteristic of enthronement psalms in the fourth book.

Hymns are more frequent in the fourth and fifth books, and certain types of reference to creation in these hymns are pervasive. As has already been shown, creation is characteristic of the enthronement hymns. The same types of references to creation that began in books one through three continue to be evident. First, God appears in a storm in Ps 97:2-5 and references to God having "established" the world appear in Pss 93:1 and 96:10. Second, Ps 95:5 praises God who "made" the sea and "formed" the land. Psalm 100 is closely related to the enthronement psalms and praises God who "made us" (verse 3). The enthronement psalms, therefore, refer to God as creating either using the imagery and language of a storm or the language of making the world. Among enthronement psalms in the fourth book, only Psalm 99 is without explicit, extensive language of creation. Even Psalm 99, however, may have some of the language and U-shaped narrative structure of the storm theophany. Peoples and Earth are called to tremble before God who comes down to Earth and appears in a "cloud" to Moses, Aaron, and Samuel (verse 6), and the psalm ends with a call to go up and worship on God's "mountain." Third, references to creation's voice (Ps 93:3) and creation's praise are ubiquitous (Pss 96:1, 11-12; 97:1, 6; 98:1, 7-8). And creation's praise of the Creator appears in the closely related Psalm 100 (verse 1).

Psalm 104 appears in the conclusion to the third book. As we have already seen, the hymns around Psalm 104 in the conclusion (Psalms 103, 105–106) show evidence of being interconnected with Psalm 104 and of understanding God as Creator acting in creation. So even some hymns like these, in which creation may not immediately seem to be present, may assume an understanding of God acting as Creator.

Psalm 104, itself, begins with a lengthy portrayal of God using the imagery and language of the storm theophany (verses 2–9). This flows into a lengthy description of blessing, fertility, and God's provision of food and life for all creatures (verses 10–30).

Most of the hymns in the fifth book include some of these same creation themes. First, creation by storm theophany occurs in a number of them. Psalm 114 praises God for the parting of the Red Sea and crossing of the Jordan with mythic language of the storm theophany. Psalm 135 praises God "who makes clouds rise" and "makes lightnings for rain" (verse 7). Psalm 147 speaks of God who "covers the skies with clouds, prepares rain for Earth" (verse 8; author translation). And Psalm 148 uses language from this tradition when it calls the sun, moon, stars, and waters above the skies to praise God, because God "established" them (verses 2–6).

Second, a number of psalms speak of God "making" or having "made" various parts of Earth. Psalm 136 praises God who "made the skies" (verse 5), "spread out Earth" (verse 6), and "made the great lights . . . sun . . . moon . . . and stars" (verses 7–9; author translation). Psalm 146:6 praises God "who made skies and Earth, the sea, and all that is in them" (author translation). And Ps 149:2 calls Israel to worship their "Maker." In addition, God is praised with the hymnic phrase "who makes skies and Earth" in a number of other genres in the fifth book.

Third, God is praised as the one who works in creation to provide food for all creatures. Psalm 111:5 praises God who "provides food." Psalm 136:25 says God "gives food to all flesh." God gives all creatures "their food" in Ps 145:15. And in Psalm 147, God "gives animals their food" (verse 9) and fills the people "with the finest of wheat" (verse 14).

Fourth, creation's praise of the Creator is an important part of these psalms. Psalm 145 prays that "all flesh will bless his holy name" (verse 21). The entire Psalm 148 is taken up with a lengthy call for all parts of Earth community to praise God. The last verse of the Psalter concludes "Let everything that breathes praise the Lord!" (150:6). This theme was also present in the enthronement hymns. Fretheim has noted that this theme is "almost exclusively associated with hymnic literature."[41] He includes a table of the biblical occurrences[42] that shows the theme occurs primarily in Psalms and second Isaiah[43] in hymns or hymnic literature. Creation's praise of the Creator is, therefore, characteristic of hymns.

In summary, certain creation images and themes appear repeatedly and are thus characteristic of hymns. First, God appears in a storm. In fact, a particular type of storm theophany is typical of hymns. The battle against the sea or historical enemies that is present when this tradition appears in other genres tends to either be in the background or altogether absent in hymns. Second, the absence of conflict coordinates well with the language and imagery of "making" skies and Earth that also appears in hymns and hymnic sections of other genres. The fact that it often appears in the participial form characteristic of hymns is an indication that this language and imagery of creation originated in, and is characteristic of, hymns. Third, the appearance of God in a storm flows naturally into the provision of blessing, fertility, and food for all creatures. Fourth, creation responds with joy and praise. These elements form an implied narrative and typical images. Therefore, God's creation by storm, making of skies and Earth, ongoing provision of fertility and food, and the joyous response of all creation are typical of hymns.

Instead of speaking of a few, isolated "creation hymns," biblical scholarship needs to recognize that creation is characteristic of hymns. Because of the importance of hymns to the book of Psalms, this means that creation is far more important to the shape and meaning of the Psalter than is often recognized, and much work needs to be done on the literary and theological meaning of creation in the Psalms.

The next two chapters will ask whether creation can support a green social and ecological vision. A recent children's movie suggests a positive answer. The second chapter of this book noted that children's literature and movies often attempt to impart values and view children as living in a Garden of Eden state close to nature. These elements are on clear view in the recent children's movie—WALL·E.[44] A reference to the Garden of Eden is prominent in the name of one of the main characters, Eve,[45] a reconnaissance robot who brings back the plant that shows the humans that Earth can once again support life. In terms of the values it teaches, the movie seems to express contemporary concerns about the amount of time children spend in front of video screens and the epidemic of childhood obesity. The humans of the future are so absorbed by the television and video chat screens constantly projected in front of their faces that they have become obese and have lost awareness of their surroundings and even of other human beings. Unlike some ecological literature, the movie has a rather sophisticated view of technology as both good and evil. Technology in the service of rampant consumerism is evil: The spaceship's computer, AUTO, who tries to prevent the humans from returning to Earth, is following the last command of the president of the corporation, Buy N Large. But, ironically, technology in the form of the robots Eve and WALL·E help humans rediscover their humanity, return to Earth, and begin to recreate Eden. The narrative reverses the plot that has humans finding salvation in heaven or, in its secular form, escaping to other planets in space, and instead has the humans return to Earth. The movie ends with the captain showing the children how to become gardeners and farmers. Clearly allusions to creation can be used in contemporary culture to reflect on social and ecological values.

CHAPTER 5

"Food to the Hungry"
HYMNS AND LIBERATION

I suspect that Walter Bruggemann reflects the suspicions of many when he argues that creation theology typically works against liberation by legitimating a fixed social order. This is an important issue for green ethics because environmentalism is sometimes an upper-class, western concern, which ignores or even is at odds with issues of poverty and human rights. My own understanding, however, is that social justice and ecological justice are interrelated and interdependent. As in the example of New Orleans, the poor are often the first to suffer from environmental disasters and the least able to recover.

Contemporary biblical scholars debate whether creation theology can support human liberation. Brueggemann has argued that creation theology tends to legitimate the current social order and works against transformation. In *Israel's Praise: Doxology against Idolatry and Ideology*, he argues that "the social function of creation theology . . .

is characteristically to establish, legitimate, and advocate order at the cost of transformation."[1] This is one point in a larger argument he makes that "the claims of royal theology want to have the 'world' of Yahweh's kingship, but without the transformative tales that are at the same time energizing and troublesome."[2] In this relation, he says, "regularly (I believe inevitably), creation theology is allied with the king, with the royal liturgy, and therefore with reasons of state" so that "the royal ordering of economic distribution and political power" is identified uncritically with "the very structure God has decreed in and for creation."[3] He recognizes that psalms may mention both creation and liberation, but thinks that when "the preponderance of words is focused on the reliability, generosity, and prosperity of the created order," it becomes less likely "that the social reality of need and scarcity will remain visible to Israel."[4]

Brueggemann's argument may seem like common sense and go unquestioned by many readers for at least two reasons. First, like Brueggemann, many readers will associate creation theology with the appeals to "natural law" that have been used against a variety of movements for human rights.[5] In contemporary society, upper-middle-class people in North America may too easily celebrate the goodness, order, and reliability of creation, and ignore the cries of the poor and marginalized and their complicity in the suffering caused by oppressive structures. Or they may focus on narrow environmental concerns to the exclusion of related issues of social justice. Brueggemann acknowledges, however, "that creation theology may indeed express a bold claim for the sovereignty of Yahweh against idols and false orderings of the world."[6] Second, Brueggemann's argument assumes a dichotomy between creation and liberation, which is similar to nature and culture and other dualisms in western thought. This paradigm, however, makes it difficult to see alternatives that may be important for overcoming the dualisms that have structured oppression in western culture. Brueggemann maintains the dualism even though he notices that creation and liberation are "nicely intertwined" in Ps 146:6-7 and that food for the hungry can be connected either with liberation (I Sam 2:5) or with the reliability of creation (Pss 104:27-28; 145:15-16).[7] In biblical literature, creation and liberation are intertwined and integrated.

While I think Brueggemann is right to be suspicious of the possible social functions of creation because of the way it has sometimes functioned, the relation of creation theology to society is a highly complex issue. First, "creation theology" is a very broad category. There are, in fact, different types and versions of creation stories in the ancient Near East and in Israel. There are, to mention just a few broad categories, stories of world creation and human creation, and original creation, and ongoing creation. Each of these may have different methods of creation. Creation may be by battle, making, commanding, or giving birth. Second, any one of these categories may have different functions in different social contexts. Richard Middleton[8] has challenged Brueggeman's argument because his experience as a theological student in the Caribbean was that creation theology was "an explosive category, profoundly liberating from otherworldly pietism and empowering for redemptive activity in a world that belongs to God."[9] Middleton appeals to "Emil Brunner who, in conversation with Karl Barth about the appeal to creation in German National Socialism, argued against Barth that creation theology was open to a variety of political uses."[10] Brunner identified a negative-conservative-authoritarian use, and positive-conservative and positive-revolutionary uses.[11] Middleton also cites the work of liberation theologian Pedro Trigo who, in his *Creation and History*, distinguishes "between creation as the conquest of chaos, a salvific event that demonizes and absolutizes two sides of a historical struggle, on the one hand, and, on the other, biblical creation faith, which relativizes both sides of this struggle *vis-à-vis* the sovereign and transcendent Creator."[12] As evidence of liberative uses of creation theology in the Bible, Middleton cites Terence Fretheim's argument that God works as Creator, in creation, to liberate the Israelites from slavery in Egypt.[13] His interpretation of the "image of God" in Gen 1:27 is that in Babylon the king was the "image of God," so Gen 1:27 is a radical democratization of the concept that "implies a radical critique of Babylonian sacral kingship and thus of the Babylonian social order which this sacral kingship legitimated."[14] I think it is generally the case that a theology or myth may have different functions in different social contexts. The doctrine of original sin, for instance, may function as a description of lived reality for a visible minority living in the inner city and function as an escape from social responsibility for white suburbanites.[15] In fact, I think it is the nature of powerful cultural stories and myths that different classes will try to use them to promote different social agendas. In summary, there are different types of creation stories, and each may have multiple social functions.

The question, therefore, would not be whether or not creation theology is opposed to liberation, but what types of creation theology, in what social contexts, might legitimate oppression or support social transformation. Brueggemann's suspicion is well founded and, as we look at the biblical evidence, we need to be wary of potentially oppressive functions of creation theologies in ancient and modern contexts. At the same time, we need to remain open to varieties of creation theology and the possibility of liberative functions in some contexts.

Contrary to Brueggemann's idea that creation supports royal theology and works against liberation, the evidence in the Psalms is that creation is repeatedly contrasted with trust in kings and associated with justice and liberation.

Psalm 33

Creation and hymns are infrequent in the first three books of the Psalter, but Psalm 33 foreshadows later parts of the Psalter when it connects creation and liberation. They appear side by side as reasons to praise God in Psalm 33:

For upright is the word [*dbr*] of the LORD;
  and his every deed is faithful.
He loves righteousness and justice;
  the LORD's steadfast love fills Earth.
By the word [*dbr*] of the LORD skies were made;
  by the breath of his mouth all their host.
He gathers in a stack the waters of the sea;
  He puts in storehouses the deeps. (verses 4–7; author translation)

The relationship of justice and creation is emphasized by the repetition of "the word of the LORD" in verses 4 and 6. God's word is "upright" and creates the world.

Contrary to Brueggemann's supposition that creation supports royal theology, praise of God as Creator is followed by a critique of government policy, military might, and kings:

The LORD frustrates the design of the nations;
  He restrains the plans of the peoples. (verse 10; author translation)

No king is saved by a great army;
  a soldier is not delivered by great strength.
War horses are a false hope for salvation,
  and by their great strength they provide no escape. (verses 16–17; author translation).

Psalm 33, therefore, combines creation, justice, and opposition to empire.

Enthronement Psalms

This combination of creation and justice reappears in the enthronement psalms and is related to their message, which is central to the message of the fourth book. The Israelites find themselves in the context of the exile without a king. Looking back on a history with many bad kings, these psalms confess that God alone is their king. This could be a subversive confession for those living under foreign empires: God is their king, not whatever human king and empire happens to be in power at the time. As discussed in the previous chapter, these psalms emphasize God as Creator so that they could be called psalms of the enthronement of God as king and Creator. Unlike many human kings, God's reign as Creator is characterized by the administration of justice. The enthronement psalms, therefore, articulate a creation theology that, far from supporting royal theology, could be subversive of human rulers and their empire building.

The absence of references to a human king in these psalms that use storm theophany imagery may be significant. The imagery and narrative pattern of the storm theophany are a major metaphor for God in the enthronement psalms (Pss 93:1-4; 96:9-11; 97:1-9; 98:7-9; 99:1, 7, 9),[16] but the battle tends to be absent or in the past, and there is no mention of a human king. This contrasts with other uses of the storm theophany where its ideological support for human kings is evident. For instance, Psalm 89 has God saying about the king:

> I will put his hand on the *sea*,
>> And his right hand on the *rivers*. (verse 25; author emphasis)

The use of sea and rivers in parallel recalls the god called Prince Sea, Judge River, who Baal defeats in Canaanite myth.[17] Earlier in Psalm 89, the same imagery is used of God who rules the sea and soothes its waves (verse 9). This imagery clearly gives the king tremendous status as *the* representative of God. This ideological connection between God as king and a human king is absent in the enthronement hymns.

In their historical and literary context, the enthronement psalms may have functioned as a critique of the type of royal theology found in Psalm 89. In other words, because God is king, the people have no need of a human king. For example, the confession that God is king has been a confession for African Americans that the president of the United States does not rule over them. Therefore, viewed against other uses of the storm theophany and creation, the lack of reference to a human king, or even God as king, may be evidence of a liberative use of creation theology.

Although kings are absent from the enthronement psalms, Psalm 99 does refer to Moses, Aaron, and Samuel (verse 6). These figures are models of the ancient priestly and prophetic leadership prior to kingship in Israel. In the context of exile and the failure of kingship, the enthronement psalms may have looked back to ancient types of leadership that could provide models for leadership in exile. Thus, the enthronement psalms may reach back behind kingship to ancient models of leadership that would provide hope for the future.

In this light, the references to God's justice may take on a new, liberative meaning. In the ancient Near Eastern ideal of the king, the king maintained justice, and this is no doubt an original source of the connection between God's reign and God's justice. But, in as much as God's justice is distanced from human kings, then God's commitment to doing justice may have potential for subverting empire.

References to God's maintenance of justice are frequent in the enthronement psalms. In Psalm 96, the call to worship is grounded in the reign of God, the stability of creation, and God's maintenance of justice:

> Say among the nations, "The Lord reigns!"
>> Surely the world is established, it shall not to be shaken,
>> He judges peoples even handedly. (verse 10; author
>>> translation)

On the one hand, this close association of kingship, justice, and stability has the potential to legitimate human monarchs. On the other hand, the emphasis on justice could be used to hold unjust rulers to account. Nevertheless, in marked contrast to the use of the imagery of God's reign elsewhere in the Hebrew Bible, no human king represents God in this psalm. God reigns alone.

In addition to distancing God's reign from human kingship, the following verses in Psalm 69 define God's reign as creation wide:

> Let the skies be glad and the earth rejoice,
>> the sea and everything that fills it thunder.
> Let the fields exult and everything in them;
>> then shall all the trees of the forest shout for joy before the
>> LORD;
> for he is coming, for he is coming to govern[18] Earth,
>> he will govern earth community with justice, and the peoples
>>> with faithfulness. (verses 9–13)

It is important to note that God's governance is just and is not limited to human justice, but extends to all creation. This is an image of God and God's justice that causes "the trees of the forest to shout for joy."

God as ruler, Creator, and justice bringer continues to be interrelated in Psalm 97. God's reign is based on justice: "Righteousness and justice are the foundation of God's throne" (verse 2). What is more, creation witnesses to justice: "The skies declare God's justice" (verse 6). This justice, rather than strength, is God's glory.

God comes in Psalm 98 to judge "Earth" with "righteousness" and "equity" (verse 9). Therefore, the enthronement psalms place God's reign and God's justice in the context of God as Creator.

Psalm 104

Psalm 104 is one of the concluding psalms of the fourth book and one of the longest creation passages in the Bible. Contrary to Brueggemann's assertion that creation theology supports "royal theology," Psalm 104 may have transformative potential in ancient and modern contexts. Compared to other biblical accounts of creation, Psalm 104 is remarkable for the lack of reference to king or temple. Against the common association of the storm theophany with kingship, the relative absence of such references in Psalm 104 is remarkable. Even though some of the imagery in the opening verses has royal connotations, Psalm 104 contrasts with psalms like Psalm 89 in that there is no mention of human kingship and with the enthronement hymns in that God is nowhere called king.

Similarly, the relation of creation to temple and the priesthood evident in some psalms—and in Genesis 1—is noticeable for its absence in Psalm 104. The narrative pattern of the storm theophany usually begins on the holy mountain and culminates in the building of the temple, and the temple or priests are mentioned in many psalms. Thomas Krüger notes that "Psalm 104 does not (at least not expressly) name the Temple as a place of mediation."[19] Karl Löning and Erich Zenger think Psalm 104 is a "deliberate counter" to some other psalms because "God's creative care is also effective and can be experienced apart from the Temple or any cultic institutionalization."[20]

Therefore, Psalm 104 is striking because of the absence of kingship, temple, and priests.

The suggestion that kingship and priesthood might be subverted by Psalm 104 is not merely an argument from silence. Verses 27 to 30 portray the direct, unmediated, and intimate relationship of God with all creatures:

> All of them wait for you
>> to give them their food in its time.
> If you give to them; they gather.
>> If you open your hand; they are well satisfied.
> If you hide your face, they are terrified;
>> If you remove their spirit/breath (*ruakh*), they perish,
>> And to their dust they return.
> If you send forth your spirit/breath (*ruakh*), they are created (*bara'*),
>> And you renew the face of the land. (author translation)

Since the same Hebrew word (*ruakh*) can be translated "breath," "wind," or "spirit," this is a portrayal of God's spirit as the life and breath of every creature. God is the spirit of life in all creation. Therefore, God's presence is not mediated by king or temple but is as close to every creature as the air they breathe.

I would submit that such direct access to the Creator is inherently subversive. One can think of many examples in history and society where marginalized people have experienced a direct relationship with the divine, and that has been perceived as threatening, dangerous, or subversive by the powers that be. "Kings" want access to God controlled through the official religion and the priests and prophets on its payroll.

Brueggemann uses the amount of specific, concrete language about justice and liberation as one of the criteria for whether creation theology and praise support social transformation. This is an important criterion in contemporary North American culture. But for ancient Israelites, living in the exile, as the defeated subjects of the Babylonian Empire, songs and writings about social transformation may have needed to be more covert. James C. Scott has written about the "hidden transcripts" that the oppressed use to express resistance and the importance of such hidden transcripts for future, overt political action.[21] I would suggest the form of creation theology in Psalm 104 could have functioned this way for Israelites in the exilic period and might continue to function this way in some contemporary contexts. We have just spoken of the subversive potential of unmediated access to the Creator. In some uses of the storm theophany, the king is the representative of the Creator who battles the earthly representatives of the spiritual forces of chaos and, thereby, becomes the conduit of blessings for the people. This clearly legitimates the king. In this context, a portrayal of access to blessings without the need for king or temple could be a hidden transcript of resistance to domination.

The picture of Leviathan in Psalm 104 may be another such hidden transcript. Political and military elites sometimes use the demonization of purported enemies to consolidate their power and mobilize the populace. Leviathan seems to have had such a function in the ancient Near East. The king was the representative of God who defended the nation against spiritual and earthly enemies. Leviathan and other primordial monsters were the symbolic or spiritual representatives of natural forces and historical enemies that threatened the well-being of the people. This is evident in passages where the military and national enemies of Israel are identified with Leviathan, Sea, or the waters. Thus, a strong and fearful picture of Leviathan would legitimate the need of a royal military machine to defend the nation. Psalm 104's portrayal of Leviathan, not as a primordial enemy of God and king, but as created by God to play in the sea—God's "rubber duckey,"[22]—could undermine royal theology and ideology. Taken together with the absence of reference to king or temple and the direct, unmediated relationship of all creatures with God, this playful representation of Leviathan as one of God's creatures could be transformative and liberating.

This symbolic concern for a just society is made more explicit in the final verse:

Let sinners disappear from Earth, and criminals be no more.
(verse 35a; author translation)

This might seem to contradict the suggestion of a hidden, symbolic transcript in Psalm 104, but the "sinners" are unnamed. It does not say let evil kings be destroyed and unjust rulers extinguished. The identity of the sinners and criminals is left to the imagination of the reader. Verse 35 could, as some have suggested, be a later addition,[23] but my interpretation suggests it has greater coherence with the rest of the psalm than commentators may have recognized. Modern readers, who do not recognize the hidden, liberative transcript, may not understand the relation of the verse to the rest of the psalm. And it may seem a negative, judgmental note on which to end a hymn. However, this verse is related to the content of the psalm, which imagines a new "paradise" in relationship to the Creator apart from empires, kings, armies, and organized religion. In considering whether creation is related to justice, not just the number of references as Brueggemann argues, but their location and integration need to be considered. The psalmist who has praised the Creator's care for all creatures and presented a vision of creation that is realistic but without need for hierarchy or oppressive rule, is convinced that the Creator's ongoing activity in creation will result in the eventual disappearance of those responsible for injustice.

This psalm was probably written in the exilic period and is in the fourth book that relates to the exile. This understanding of creation, then, comes in the context of great suffering. First northern Israel, and then Judah, had invading armies lay siege to their cities. They experienced the atrocities of war and eventual humiliation and defeat. Many prominent citizens were taken in chains into exile and had to start from nothing in a foreign land. They had confessed and believed that God would fight for them and protect Zion and the temple, but the harsh realities of war seemed to have proven the gods of their enemies to be superior. Nevertheless, after all the personal and national laments in the book of Psalms that express their suffering and harsh reality that have lead up to this point in the book, they have discovered the steadfast love and power of God in the goodness and reliability of creation. Israel has experienced national chaos and, on the other side of chaos, is able to see that chaos (Leviathan) has a place in creation. They recognize humans as an integral part of a creation cared for by the Creator. They recognize the dangers of identifying God and king and have an understanding of relationship to God as Creator apart from and perhaps in opposition to empire. Similarly, in contemporary contexts of empire, Psalm 104 may have potential for imagining a world of social and ecological justice.

Justice in Psalms 145–150

Moving into the fifth book of the Psalter, Psalms 145–150 continue to relate creation and justice and have a prominent location as the conclusion to the Psalter. They are all hymns with creation themes, and Psalm 145 is the last of a collection of psalms of David. Several connect creation and justice.

Creation and justice are intertwined in Psalm 145. Psalm 145:7 characterizes God's reign in terms of good governance and the administration of justice (*tsdaqah*). This conception of God's reign may come from the ancient Near Eastern understanding of a just king, but God rules as Creator. God as Creator provides food for all creatures:

> The eyes of all look to you,
>> and you give them their food in due season.
> You open your hand,
>> satisfying the desire of every living thing. (verses 15–16)

These verses are preceded and followed by verses that speak of justice. The preceding verse talks of God's work against oppression:

> The LORD upholds all who are falling,
>> and raises up all who are bowed down. (verse 14)

The verses that follow the provision of food in creation, speak of God's justice:

> The LORD is just [*tsaddiq*] in all his ways,
>> and kind in all his doings [*ma'ase*].
> The LORD is near to all who call on him,
>> to all who call on him in truth.
> He fulfills the desire of all who fear him;
>> he also hears their cry, and saves them.
> The LORD watches over all who love him,
>> but all the wicked he will destroy. (verses 17–20)

The word used of God's "doings" (*ma'ase*), is that same word that has been used of God's acts in creation elsewhere in the Psalms and, in the immediate context, refers back to the provision of food, so God's "doings" as Creator and justice continue to be intertwined in verse 17. This verse and the following verses praise God as just, responding to the cries of those in distress and destroying the wicked. Thus, one could say that the Creator's provision of food is integrated into the creation and maintenance of justice.

In the heart of Psalm 146, there is a verse that links the provision of food and the maintenance of justice:

> who executes justice [*mishpat*] for the oppressed;
>> who gives food to the hungry. (verse 7a)

As in Psalm 145, Psalm 146 links the Creator's provision of food with justice. Again the verses that surround this verse reinforce the connection between creation and justice. The verse is preceded by verses that speak of the happiness of those whose "help" and "hope" (verse 5) is in God as Creator:

> who makes skies and Earth,
>> the sea, and all that is in them;
> who keeps faith forever. (verse 6; author translation)

Psalm 146, verse 7, which speaks of the provision of food, is the beginning of a substantial and detailed confession of God's work as liberator:

> The LORD sets the prisoners free;
>> the LORD opens the eyes of the blind.
> The LORD lifts up those who are bowed down;
>> the LORD loves the righteous.
> The LORD watches over the strangers;
>> he upholds the orphan and the widow,
>> but the way of the wicked he brings to ruin. (verses 7b–9)

Even Brueggemann acknowledges that this psalm speaks concretely of justice in the context of creation. He uses nearby psalms to argue that creation has a tendency to forget the "transformative tales that are at the same time energizing and troublesome."[24] But, if these psalms have been edited to be read together, the presence of this psalm in the conclusion of the Psalter, among other psalms that speak of creation and justice, insists that creation and justice can and should be held together.

In the ancient Near East, these are functions of the ideal king, and the concluding verse celebrates God's reign. Fredric Jameson, the American, Marxist, literary critic, has made the point that the ideological vision of the ruling class needs to portray a "popular front," which includes the ideologies of other classes. Yet these elements taken from the ideologies of other classes are bills that can come due and be used by other classes to assert their interests against the dominant ideology.[25] Something like this may be happening in this psalm, because God's kingship is distanced from human kingship in the immediately preceding verses:

> Do not put your trust in princes,
>> in mortals, in whom there is no help.
> When their breath departs, they return to Earth;[26]
>> on that very day their plans perish. (146:3-4)

With these verses, God's kingship is distanced from human kingship and, in the following verses, placed in the broader context of God's work as Creator in creation. God acts not through a human king's political and military plans, but in creation. In the context of the exile and restoration of Israel, this theology would mean that the Creator of skies and Earth does not need to raise up a king and military leader for Israel, but is able to work through a foreign ruler, Cyrus, to allow the Israelites to return to their homeland and rebuild the temple. Creation and liberation are integrated and distanced from human kingship. God rules, but rules as Creator and liberator.

Psalm 147 is divided into three sections by calls to worship: "Praise the LORD" in verse 1, "Sing to the LORD with thanksgiving;

make melody to our God on the lyre" in verse 7, and "Praise the LORD, O Jerusalem! Praise your God, O Zion!" in verse 12. In each of the sections, God is active as both Creator and liberator.

In the first section (verses 1–6), the reasons for praise include God's work gathering the outcasts of Israel, healing emotional and physical wounds, determining the number and names of stars, and working for justice in the world. It is the Creator who "determines the number of the stars," (verse 4) and:

> The LORD lifts up the downtrodden;
>> he casts the wicked to the ground. (verse 6)

The power of God as Creator to determine the number of the stars (verses 4–5) is central to God's work of gathering (verse 2), healing (verse 3), and working for justice in the world (verse 6).

The second section (verses 7–10) sings of God's work in creation at some length. God is the source of the rain essential for the fertility of the land and the provision of food for all creatures (verses 8–9). Along with the presence of God in rain storms come several hints of a relationship between creation and justice and liberation. While God appears in a rain storm, this is connected not with a military battle, as is often the case with storm theophanies, but with the provision of the rain necessary for food. Since the provision of food for all creatures is associated with justice in the previous psalm, it may have connotations of God's justice in this psalm. Moreover, the following verse says that God's "delight is not in the strength of the horse" (verse 10a). Since the horse was associated with war in the ancient Near East, this statement may subvert the underpinnings of empire by distancing God from military might and placing God squarely in the realm of creation providing fertility and food.

The association of God with storms is elaborated in a different and even lengthier manner in the third section of Psalm 147 (verses

11–20). God works as Creator, blessing children, providing food, and sending snow, hail, wind, and water. Again, God's presence in storms is not associated with battle. Significant also, is that the blessing of children is associated with security in verse 13 and good food with peace in verse 14:

> For he strengthens the bars of your gates;
>> he blesses your children within you.
> He grants peace within your borders;
>> he fills you with the finest of wheat.

The blessing of children would mean numerous, strong, healthy children. These children then are the source of security for cities. Similarly, peace is connected with good food for everyone. While fortifications are mentioned at the beginning of verse 13 and the children may become soldiers, the verses seem to recognize that true and enduring security and peace are achieved, not by military might, but more fundamentally by the provision of food and health for all. In modern parlance, the military cannot bring peace without social and economic development.

The concluding verses of the third and final section of Psalm 147 make a connection between God's word in creation and God's word to Israel. Note the parallel uses of God's word:

> He sends out his command to Earth;[27]
>> his *word* runs swiftly.
> He gives snow like wool;
>> he scatters frost like ashes.
> He hurls down hail like crumbs—
>> who can stand before his cold?
> He sends out his *word*, and melts them;
>> he makes his wind blow, and the waters flow.

He spoke his *word*[28] to Jacob,

his statutes and judgments[29] to Israel

He has not dealt thus with any other nation;

they do not know his judgments.

Praise the LORD! (verses 15–20).

God's *word* to Earth, snow, frost, wind and waters, is parallel to God's *word* to Israel. The Hebrew words translated "statutes and judgments" (verse 19), are used frequently in Deuteronomy and the Deuteronomistic history.[30] The primary meaning of "judgments" is decisions in a court of law. In this psalm, God's words in a court of justice are placed in parallel with God's words in creation, so that the social and religious instructions that have been given to Israel are related to the laws of creation. The understanding of justice given in Israel is related to and extends to the order of nature, so creation and justice are related.

To summarize, references to justice and liberation are not as concrete as in Psalm 146, but Psalm 147 continues to assume a relationship between creation and justice. Creation is mentioned in the first section, and each of the second and third sections uses imagery of God's presence in a storm. This creation imagery is then related to God's intervention on behalf of the oppressed (verse 6), which is distanced from military intervention (horses), and based, instead, on the food, security, and health necessary for lasting peace. Finally, God's word about justice in Israel is placed in parallel to God's word in creation. So creation and justice continue to be interrelated in Psalm 147.

Psalm 148 calls all parts of creation to praise God. Among those called to praise God are sun, moon, stars (verse 3), hail, snow, frost, mountains, hills, trees, animals, and birds (verses 8–10). The reason they should praise God is introduced by the word "for," as is typical in hymns (verses 5 and 13). The reason is that God is their Creator. God "created (*bara'*) . . . established them forever and ever" (verses 5–6). Brueggemann thinks that the lack of concrete reference to liberation in this psalm is an indication that creation theology forgets the cry of the oppressed and supports the status quo. This overlooks the fact that Psalm 148 is one of a group of hallelujah psalms, connected together by the use of that word at the beginning, end, and sometimes in the middle of these psalms. In addition, the absence of superscriptions is an indication these psalms have been placed as a conclusion to the Psalter. Psalm 148 comes after Psalms 146 and 147, which integrate creation and justice, and comes before Psalm 149, which is very much concerned with justice.

The manner in which that concern for justice is expressed in Psalm 149 may be disturbing for those concerned with the history of violence done in the name of religion. The psalm calls Israel to "be glad in its Maker" in verse 2, and then verses 6–9 say:

> Let the high praises of God be in their throats
>> and two-edged swords in their hands,
> to execute vengeance on the nations
>> and punishment on the peoples,
> to bind their kings with fetters
>> and their nobles with chains of iron,
> to enact among them the justice which is written.[31]
>> This is glory for all his faithful ones.

What are we to make of these verses? These verses were cited to call Roman Catholic princes to holy war against Protestants at the beginning of the Thirty Years War and by Thomas Müntzer to incite German peasants to revolt.[32] J. Clinton McCann concludes that taking these verses literally is "positively dangerous" and advocates reading them figuratively.[33] While I would largely agree, I recognize that as a person who holds a privileged position within the contemporary, global economy, I have a vested interest in opposition to violence that might upset the status quo. I may conveniently overlook the depth and extent of the suffering caused by an economy that supports my lifestyle and the state-sanctioned military and police violence that maintain current economic arrangements. Those living under an oppressive, colonial rule, as the Israelites did, and as many contemporary peoples do, may have a much different perception. For them, violence may be the only way to overcome evil, restore justice, and build a lasting peace. Although "peoples" are mentioned in verse 7, the focus is on "nations" (verse 7) and their leaders (verse 8), so one could say that the passage speaks of the end of rulers and nations that oppress. And even if we cannot agree with these verses on a literal level, we can recognize a passion for justice, which is related to God as Creator. The praise of God as "Maker" is closely related to the end of political hierarchies that oppress and the coming of justice.

Therefore, Psalms 145, 146, 147, and 149 frequently and in a variety of ways relate creation to issues of justice. So the Psalter concludes with psalms expressing a creation theology that, far from being in denial, express a concern for justice and liberation.

CHAPTER 6

"Let Earth Rejoice"

ECOJUSTICE IN HYMNS

The previous chapter showed that creation theologies in the Psalter could support liberation. However, creation theology is not necessarily ecological. As Norman Habel says, "an appeal to creation theology in a given biblical text or tradition does not necessarily imply a genuine ecological concern for Earth or creation."[1] I think Habel is right to be suspicious of creation theologies, because some creation theologies in the Psalms are not Earth friendly. This chapter, however, will show that creation theology in the Psalms can be ecological and support ecojustice. For lack of a better term, I often use the word *ecojustice* to refer to this interrelationship of social and ecological justice.

Voice and Intrinsic Value of Earth

The Introduction discussed the ecojustice principles of the Earth Bible project. These principles for interpreting the Bible were developed by an international team of biblical scholars and theologians in dialogue with ecologists. Among the principles were intrinsic worth, interconnectedness, voice, and identification. These ecojustice principles are found in hymns that speak of God as Creator.

The discussion of the role of hymns and creation in the Psalter noted that a cluster of enthronement hymns (Psalms 93, 95–99) are centrally located in the fourth book and are central to its message. Because these hymns frequently speak of creation, creation is central to the shape and message of the fourth book. Several of these enthronement hymns include in their creation theology an understanding of creation that corresponds to ecojustice principles. From an ecological perspective, these psalms are significant because they identify God with creation, and creation is alive, active, interrelated, and has intrinsic worth and a voice. In addition, they play an important role in the shape and message of the fourth book of the Psalter.

Psalm 93

Beginning in Psalm 93, the reader encounters creation speaking. The first two verses place the stability of the world in parallel with the stability of God's throne. The natural world can be counted on because God is king. Then creation speaks:

> The tides[2] have lifted up, O Lord,
>> The tides have lifted up their voice,
> The tides have lifted up their pounding.
>> Above the thunder of might waters,
> more majestic than the breakers of the sea,
>> majestic is the Lord on high. (verses 3–4; author translation)

The psalm does not tell the reader what the tides are saying. Since the word translated "tides" is the same word that is used as one of the names of Baal's adversary, Sea, in Ugaritic myth, it would be natural in the context of the ancient Near East to think of the powers of chaos that threaten world order. Although this psalm does not tell us what the tides say, they seem to represent the ongoing threats to the order of creation that are, nevertheless, controlled by the Creator.

Psalm 95

In the following psalms, this potentially threatening voice is transformed into praise of God. Psalm 95 praises God as rock and Creator of sea, land, and people. It opens with a call to praise the "Rock":

> Come, let us cry for joy to the LORD,
>> raise a shout for the Rock of our salvation. (Ps 95:1; author
>> translation)

This is followed by praise of God as Creator of the world (verses 4–5) and humanity (verse 6). Since the metaphor for God that opens the psalm is God as rock, it is possible to think of the Rock as the Creator of world and humanity. This metaphor for the Creator identifies God with creation. The psalm speaks of the Creator not as separate from nature, but as part of nature. Indeed, rock forms the core of Earth; land is created by the molten rock of volcanoes and soil by erosion of rock. Plants and animals are made of minerals, and life depends on minerals that come from the soil.[3]

Next, the imagery of creation is followed by pastoral imagery (verse 7). God is a shepherd involved in the earthy business of herding sheep, and the human speakers in the psalm identify with sheep. So this is alternate imagery for God in Earth and the identification of humans with other Earth creatures.

Although the imagery for God has shifted to God as shepherd, if the reader continues to treat *Rock* as the governing metaphor for

God, as in the Rock is also Shepherd, then the exclamation in the same verse—"Now if only you would listen to his voice"—could be understood as asking the reader to listen to the Rock. The verses that follow about the people testing God at Massah and Meribah refer to stories of God bringing water from *rock*.[4] Psalm 95 says they tested God, even though they had seen God's work (verse 9). The work of God that they had seen is also God's work in nature. The so-called plagues and the deliverance from the Egyptians at the sea by wind and water were God's presence in creation. The psalm ends by warning that those who do not listen to the voice of God as rock and Creator in nature will not enter into divine rest (*mnukhah*). This word that ends the psalm has connotations of rest at the end of a journey and peace. Those who do not listen to the voice of the Creator in creation will not enter into God's physical and spiritual rest. Thus, this psalm begins with an image of God as rock, a part of creation, and is about creation and the Creator's presence in nature. It identifies God and humanity with Earth and can be understood as calling readers to listen to the voice of God as rock in creation. This, then, is an ecological, creation theology!

Psalm 96

Psalm 95 calls people to listen to the voice of the Creator in Earth, and in Psalm 96 the voice of Earth is raised in praise of the Creator. Psalm 96 calls "all Earth" (verse 1; author translation) to praise God. Unlike the idols, God has "made the skies" (verse 5; author translation). Whereas the pounding of the surf threatened Earth in Psalm 93, now it is called to worship and dance before God:

> Worship the Lord in sacred glory;
>> Dance[5] before him all Earth . . . (verse 9; author translation)

Let the skies be glad and Earth rejoice,

> the sea and everything that fills it thunder.

Let the fields exult and everything in them;

> then shall all the trees of the forest shout for joy before the
> Lord.

(verses 11–12; author translation)

Earth is addressed as a living subject with a voice, capable of responding to God with dancing and shouts of joy. Terence Fretheim thinks that "nature's praise of God is to be understood and explicated" in the context of the use of natural metaphors for God, like *rock* in Psalm 95. He recognizes that all metaphors for God have an "is" and an "is not" relation to God. If, however, natural metaphors are in some sense a description of God, then "they reflect in their very existence, in their being what they are, the reality which is God." This speaks to him of their intrinsic value.[6] Therefore, Psalm 96 speaks of the voice and intrinsic worth of creation.

Psalms 97 and 98

God as ruler, Creator, and justice bringer continue to be interrelated in Psalm 97. This psalm is not without its problems for an environmentalist. The violence toward Earth of the traditional imagery of the storm god is strong in this psalm. God comes in dark clouds and "fire goes before God and consumes God's enemies on every side" (verse 3; author translation). God is portrayed as high above Earth—"Most High over all Earth" (verse 9; author translation)—and wreaks fear and destruction on some parts of Earth community—"mountains melt like wax before the Lord" (verse 5). In addition, God's help seems to be directed only to humans (verses 8, 10–12). This could legitimate an anthropology that sees humanity as separate from and above nature and an anthropocentric understanding of God's work focused solely on the salvation of humans.

Nevertheless, Psalm 97 does begin with a call for all Earth to rejoice, and the islands to be glad (verse 1; author translation). So Earth is addressed as alive and assumed to have a voice, and one part of Earth community speaks: "The skies declare God's justice" (verse 6; author translation). Earth is addressed as a subject, and Earth and skies have a voice.

The voice of sea that was ominous in Psalm 93, and turned into rejoicing in Ps 96:9, becomes praise in Psalm 98. Once again "all Earth" is called to praise the Creator (verse 4; author translation). First humans are called to praise with song, lyre, trumpet, and horns (verses 5–6). Then sea, Earth community (*tevel*), tides (*nharot*), and hills are called to join in with roaring, clapping, and singing (verses 7–8). Whereas the mountains melted with fear in the previous psalm, now they "sing together for joy" (verse 8).

How can the Earth community praise God? Does the imagery force other creatures into a human mold? The hymns do not provide an answer, but Psalm 65, a community thanksgiving, does. Thanksgiving is on the way from lament to hymns, so Psalm 65 has a close relationship to hymns. Psalm 65 says:

> The pastures of the wilderness overflow,
>> the hills gird themselves with joy,
> the meadows clothe themselves with flocks,
> the valleys deck themselves with grain,
>> they shout and sing together for joy. (verses 12–13)

Howard Wallace notes that the parallelism of the lines "makes clear that an abundance of flocks and crops is the means by which the pastures and hills rejoice." He concludes that this broadens the understanding of praise. "Life itself, which is lived in fullness, wholeness and peace, is an offering of joy and praise to the God whose gift that life is."[7]

This movement toward all creation praising God foreshadows a similar movement at the end of the book of Psalms.

Psalm 104

The enthronement psalms are central to the fourth book and Psalm 104 is an important part of the conclusion to this book, Psalms 103–106. In comparison to the more famous versions of creation in Genesis 1–3, Psalm 104 is far more ecological. The depiction of the role of humanity in creation is less anthropocentric than Genesis 1–3. Humans appear in only four of the twenty-one verses (verses 14–15, 23, 35). One could argue that more verses are dedicated to the humans than any other creature, that they appear in central verses, and that the other parts of creation provide for them. Yet, in contrast to Genesis, there is no mention of humans being made in the image of God, or having a special, royal role of dominion over other creatures.[8] Humans, like all other creatures, are dependant on the spirit of God for life (verses 29–30) and depend on water and Earth to produce the plants they need for food (verses 13–14). In contrast to Genesis 1–3, therefore, humans are just one of many creatures cared for and sustained by the Creator.

Moreover, there are creatures and parts of creation in the passage that seem to have intrinsic value independent of humans. A whole chain of relationships leads up to and supports the birds singing in the trees (verses 10–12).[9] God provides for a variety of animals that live in remote areas, have no particular value for humans, and may even be dangerous. God provides drink for wild animals and wild asses (verse 11). Young lions "[seek] their food from God" (verse 21). Mountains and rocks provide habitats and refuge for wild goats and coneys (verse 18). The exclamation—"Leviathan that you formed to play in it" (verse 26; author translation)—is striking and representative of wild and dangerous animals that have intrinsic value in creation. Even the primordial monster Leviathan, who elsewhere represents the forces of chaos that God battles, has a valued place in creation.

This ancient celebration of Creator and creation has similarities to modern ecology's understanding of the interrelationship and interdependence of all species in the web of life. While the number of species named is limited, the passage does, by the species it chooses to mention, represent in symbolic, poetic form the abundance and diversity of species and their interdependence. The species represented move from mountains to valleys, up into the mountains again, and then out to sea. They include domestic animals that humans need and animals that are of no use—like wild goats and rock coneys—or are dangerous to humans—like lions. Thus habitats and species are chosen to represent a world of diverse habitats teeming with creatures or, in the language of praise and awe, "How manifold are your works. . . . earth is full of your creatures" (Ps 104:24). While all the complex interrelationships are not portrayed, enough chains of life are traced in poetic form to indicate the interrelationship and interdependence of various species and their habitats. Springs provide water for wild animals and wild asses (verses 10–12). Springs flow into streams that water trees (verses 12, 16), which, in turn, provide habitat for storks and other birds (verses 12, 17). Mountains provide habitat for wild goats and the rocks for wild coneys (verse 18). The sea provides habitats for "creeping things" (verse 25). In these ways, the poetry portrays a world similar to that described by modern ecology—abundant, diverse, interrelated, and interdependent.

Christian theologies have often understood the goodness of creation emphasized in Genesis 1 as largely undone by Genesis 2–3. This

North Atlantic interpretation of creation as largely evil has facilitated the exploitation of women, indigenous peoples, and Earth. This is certainly not the view of Psalm 104. Although the word "good" itself is only used once (verse 28), Psalm 104 is a celebration of the continuing goodness of creation. Genesis 3:14-19 dwells on what is cursed, but Ps 104:10-30 places curse in the broader context of goodness and blessing.[10] In Gen 3:14, the serpent is cursed and has to crawl on its belly, but in Ps 104:26, the serpent Leviathan[11] is created to frolic in the sea. Genesis 3:17 says the land is cursed on account of humanity, but Ps 104:30 recognizes that the land is continually renewed by the spirit of God. In Gen 3:17-18, the land produces thorns and thistles, and humans have to work hard to eke out a living; in Ps 104:30, the spirit of God renews the land, and, in verse 14, God causes plants to grow and serve humans by bringing forth bread and wine (verse 15). The mention of bread and wine suggests not just enough to eat, but good food and good times. The poetry portrays creation as full of beauty and joy. That a chain of events leads up to the singing of the birds suggests that these songs are for the enjoyment of other creatures.[12] The portrayal of Leviathan playing in the sea suggests that play and enjoyment are built into creation. The psalmist even prays that God will *rejoice* or *take pleasure* in the world (verse 31). Far from being cursed, creation has goodness and blessing that includes a sense of beauty and joy.

This is not a naïve or romantic understanding of the created world. As Miller notes, the psalm recognizes that nature is "red in tooth and claw" and "incorporates the understanding of a food chain that pits animal against animal."[13] The Creator's care for all creatures includes providing prey for lions (verse 21). Or as Löning and Zenger note, "the psalm is aware of the perils of life in this world."[14] Although the order of creation is emphasized, the primeval waters of chaos can still be experienced in the present when the waters stand above the mountains in clouds and fall as rain to rush down the mountains in torrents (verses 8–13). The shaking and smoking of the mountains at the end of the psalm (verse 32) is an experience of the Creator continually maintaining order as at the beginning. On the human level, chaos is the day to day presence of criminals in society that the last verse of the psalms prays will one day disappear. Finally, "when you take away their breath, they die" (verse 29) recognizes the utter dependence of life on God.[15]

Psalm 104 is remarkable because a direct relationship with God extends not just to humans, but to all species. Psalm 104 says the lions "*seek* their food from God" (verse 21; author translation) and that all creatures "*wait* for you to give them their food" (verse 27; author translation). The Hebrew words translated *seek* and *wait* have broad ranges of meaning, but they include seeking God's presence and hoping in God. Thus, one could say that the lions, and indeed all creatures, are pictured as praying to God. This corroborates the previously mentioned image of God's spirit as the force of life present in all creatures (verses 29–30) so that all creatures have an unmediated relationship with God. In contemporary society, where exploitation of creation is founded on the assumption that humans are superior to other species, this image of God's presence in all life could support a vision of ecological liberation that is interrelated with human liberation.

Psalms 145–150

This emphasis on the intrinsic worth and voice of creation continues in the fifth book and comes to a crescendo in the psalms that conclude the Psalter. Psalm 145 says, "All your works shall give thanks to you, O LORD" (verse 10). In the context, "works" refers to all created things. And Psalm 145 concludes with "all flesh will bless his holy name" (verse 21). Psalm 148, which stands as the center and climax of these concluding hymns, is a lengthy call for many parts of creation to praise God:

> Praise him, all his angels;
>> praise him, all his host!
> Praise him, sun and moon;
>> praise him, all you shining stars!
> Praise him, you highest heavens,
>> and you waters above the heavens!
> Let them praise the name of the LORD,
>> for he commanded and they were created.
> He established them forever and ever;
>> he fixed their bounds, which cannot be passed.
> Praise the LORD from the earth,
>> you sea monsters and all deeps,
> fire and hail, snow and frost,
>> stormy wind fulfilling his command!
> Mountains and all hills,
>> fruit trees and all cedars!
> Wild animals and all cattle,
>> creeping things and flying birds! (verses 2–10)

Psalms 149 and 150 call Israel to take part in all creation's praise of God and work for justice. Psalm 150:6, the final verse of the final psalm concludes: "Let everything that breathes praise the LORD! Praise the LORD!" Creation's praise of the Creator appears occasionally earlier in the Psalter (Psalms 19; 65; 69:34), builds through the Psalter (Psalms 96, 98, 100), and comes to a climax in these concluding hymns. Creation is a subject that is alive with a voice and intrinsic worth. Therefore, creation's praise plays a key role in the final form of the Psalter and is ecological.

Ecojustice

In addition to supporting human liberation, as the previous chapter showed, the Psalter's hymns connect creation theology with an understanding of justice that extends to all creation. *Justice* refers in the creation theology of the Psalter's hymns, not only to humans, but to all creation, so that the understanding of justice is social and ecological.

The enthronement psalms are central to the meaning and message of the fourth book. They combine God as Creator with ecojustice. Psalm 96, for instance, combines God as Creator with creation's praise and justice for all creatures.

> Say among the nations, "The Lord reigns!"
>> Surely the world is established, it shall not to be shaken,
>> He judges peoples even handedly.
> Let the skies be glad and Earth rejoice,
>> the sea and everything that fills it thunder.
> Let the fields exult and everything in them;
>> then shall all the trees of the forest shout for joy;
> Before the Lord, for he is coming[16] to govern[17] Earth,
>> he will govern Earth community with justice,
>> and the peoples with faithfulness. (verses 10–13; author translation)

The statement in verse 10 that "the world is established, it shall not be shaken" is language from the tradition of the storm theophany. It is followed immediately by a statement about God's administration of justice. There are a number of ways the placement of these two lines together could be explained, but the poetry does not provide the logic. As much as can be said with certainty in this context is that creation is closely related to God's justice. This statement about justice is then followed by calls for various parts of Earth community to praise God (verses 11–12). In this case, the poetry does provide the logic. As is typical of hymns, the reason for praise is preceded by "for." The various parts of Earth community are called to praise because God is coming to govern with justice. The Hebrew word usually translated "world" can mean the peoples of the world, the inhabited world, or the whole world and is often in parallel to Earth as it is here. I have translated it "Earth community," because, in this context, it refers to all parts of Earth that are called to praise God. But why would they praise God, unless God's just governance was in some measure good for them? This is an image of God and God's justice that causes "the trees of the forest [to] shout for joy." God governs with justice and that justice is not limited to human justice but extends to all creation.

Similarly, in Psalm 97, God's governance is characterized by justice: "righteousness and justice are the foundation of his throne" (verse 2). Once again, this statement about God's justice is nestled in the midst of imagery of God's appearance in a storm, so the two, creation and justice, are intimately related. This is a justice in which all creation takes part, because Earth is called to rejoice: "Let Earth rejoice, many islands be glad!" (verse 1; author translation), and "the skies declare God's justice" (verse 6; author translation). Earth and skies take part in praising God's justice and teaching justice. Presumably, then, this is a justice that includes them and is part of the warp and woof of the living fabric of creation.

The passage from Psalm 97 just quoted is closely parallel to another passage in Psalm 98:

Shout for the Lord, all Earth,
  break into cries of joy and sing. . . .
Let the sea and all that fills it thunder,
  Earth community and those who live in it

> Let tides clap their hands,
>> Let the hills shout for joy together before the LORD.
> For he is coming to govern Earth,
>> He will govern Earth community with justice,
>> and peoples even handedly. (verses 4, 7–9; author translation)

Once again, many parts of Earth community are called to rejoice, and the reason for praise is God's justice. The Hebrew of Ps 98:9 is almost identical to Ps 96:13. All creatures are subjects of God's just reign so that social justice is included in the broader framework of ecological justice.

Expressions of ecojustice also appear in the hymns that conclude the Psalter.

Psalm 145 says:

> The LORD upholds all who are falling,
>> and raises up all who are bowed down.
> The eyes of all look to you,
>> and you give them their food in due season.
> You open your hand,
>> satisfying the desire of every living thing.
> The LORD is just [tsaddiq] in all his ways,
>> and kind in all his doings [ma'asav]. (verses 14–17)

God's provision of food (verses 13–16) is surrounded by statements about God working for justice (verse 14) and acting justly (verse 17). By providing food, God is also working for justice. Since all creatures are included, God's justice extends to all creation.

While not quite as explicit, a similar understanding of creational justice may lie behind Psalm 147. God is present in creation controlling the clouds and rains for the plants that provide food for animals:

He covers the heavens with clouds,
    prepares rain for the earth,
    makes grass grow on the hills.
He gives to the animals their food,
    and to the young ravens when they cry. (verses 8–9)

As in Psalm 145, the provision of food is sandwiched between statements about God's justice. Psalm 147:6 says,

The Lord lifts up the downtrodden;
    he casts the wicked to the ground.

And 147:10 says,

[God's] delight is not in the strength of the horse,
    nor his pleasure in the speed of a runner.

Since the horse was a weapon of war, this could be understood as subverting military claims to divine authorization. Even if God's provision of food were not placed in the immediate context of statements about God's justice, a reader might hear the statement in Psalm 147 about God providing food for animals in the context of the similar statement in Psalm 145, where it is part of God's work for justice, because the two psalms have been placed together as a conclusion to the Psalter.

The concluding verses of this section and Psalm 147 make a connection between God's word in creation and God's word in prophecy and scripture. Note the two parallel uses of God's word:

[God] sends out his *word*, and melts them;
    he makes his wind blow, and waters flow.
He spoke his *word*[18] to Jacob,
    his statutes and judgments to Israel. (verses 18–19; author
       translation)

God's word in creation is parallel to God's word to Jacob. The expression "statutes and judgments" is frequently used in Deuteronomy and the Deuteronomistic history.[19] The primary meaning of *judgments* is decisions in a court of law. The understanding of justice given in Israel is related to, and extends to, the order of nature.

Therefore, these hymns show a number of signs of a concept of ecojustice. First, creation celebrates because the Creator is coming to bring justice to all creation. Second, divine justice includes the provision of food for all creatures. Third, God's word is manifest in creation and in the "statutes and judgments" of Israel, so ecology and society are in some sense related. Because these hymns appear at important locations for the final form of the Psalter, they make a contribution both to the implied narrative of hymns and to the story of the Psalter as a whole, which will be discussed in the following sections.

Imagery and Implied Narrative

Because creation is characteristic of hymns, it contributes to their typical imagery and implied narrative. Admittedly, creation does not appear in every hymn, but then not every element typical of a genre appears in every particular occurrence of that genre. Creation occurs in enough hymns to say that it is typical of hymns. At least by the end of the Psalter and the biblical period, God's activity as Creator in creation came to be characteristic of hymns. This study is particularly interested in what kind of world these recurring images and narrative patterns envision and whether that world imagines a helpful, ecological vision of the future. The hymns are a large and diverse genre, and I will not attempt here an exhaustive description of the imagery and implied narrative of the hymn but will focus only on those elements related to creation and ecology.

The recurring imagery and narrative of creation creates a typical story. God has created the world. The imagery of God's appearance in a storm to establish order is the most common way of describing creation.[20] This pattern uses typical vocabulary of "founding" and "establishing" the world so that, when this vocabulary appears, it may allude to the imagery of God's approach in a storm to establish order and fertility (Ps 96:10). Other modes of world creation appear less frequently. They include creation by word (Ps 33:4-9) and creation by God's spirit (Ps 104:29-30).

Other than the storm theophany, the most common language for God's creation of the world is "making" or "forming." In the fifth book, the expression, "who makes heaven and earth," and similar phrases appear frequently. This language seems to assume a metaphor of God as builder or craftsperson. While the metaphor is not made explicit in Psalms, it is made explicit in other biblical books (Prov 8:27-29, Job 38:4-6). This same language is used for human creation, which also appears in hymns. God makes the world, and God makes human beings (Pss 33:15; 95:6; 100:3; 103:14).

Creation is not only about a beginning, but is ongoing. God continues to be active as Creator in creation (Ps 104:29-30). The Creator continues to provide blessing and fertility for the land (Pss 29:11; 104:10-30). The storm in which God appears brings the rain that is necessary for the fertility of the land, so it is logical that hymns often mention that God provides water and food for all creatures.[21]

God also works as Creator in nature to deliver the Israelites from slavery in Egypt. The plagues are natural disorders. God divides the sea, which recalls the ancient Near Eastern myth, and provides food and water in the wilderness.

As in the exodus story, we have seen that hymns make a connection between God's provision of food and water for the poor with God's work for justice in the world. God has created a world with a just order, is continually at work to maintain justice, and is coming to judge the world.[22] God's steadfast love is evident in the stability of creation and provision of food, water, and fertility for all creatures.

Because God has created the world and everything in it, God rules the world. Moreover, God rules the world as Creator working in creation. This is particularly evident in the enthronement psalms. Of course, this way of telling the story places God's reign in the broader context of creation. I do this intentionally because I think the kingship of God has been extensively discussed and emphasized in the scholarly literature, and I want to highlight what has been less often discussed and emphasized, the imagery of God as Creator. As this discussion has made evident, God rules the world because God has created it and continues to work in creation, maintaining justice and life for all creatures.

In response to God's rule as Creator, Earth responds with joy. Creation is alive and has a voice. The heavens declare the glory and righteousness of God (Pss 19:1; 97:6). All Earth community is called to respond with joy and praise. Their joy is expressed by doing what they do naturally (Ps 65:12-13).

Humans are called to come to the house of God on the holy mountain where they take part in all creation's praise of the Creator.[23] The narrative moves both toward the temple as humans come up to join in the worship and toward the integration of humans into creation as they join in harmony with creation's celebration.

The Psalter recognizes that evil continues to exist in the world, but looks with hope for a new age of peace and harmony among all creatures.

In summary, God has created the world and continues to create everything in it. God rules the world with steadfast love and justice that is manifest in creation. God raises up the oppressed and provides food, water, blessing, and fertility for all creatures. Because evil continues in the world, this is a prophetic hope that justice, abundant life, and peace for all creatures will eventually prevail. Creation responds with joy, and humans come to the temple to take part in creation's praise of the Creator.

The Psalter's Story

Creation makes an important contribution to the Psalter's story, because creation is characteristic of hymns, and they appear at key locations in the final form of the Psalter. Hymns become more frequent towards the end of the Psalter, and creation is typical of hymns. This means that towards the end of the Psalter, as the frequency of hymns increases, so do representations of God as Creator.

In addition to more frequent appearances toward the end of the Psalter, hymns to God as Creator appear in key locations in the Psalter. God as Creator is pervasive in the enthronement psalms, which are central to the message of the fourth book. Briefly, the monarchy has been a failure, but Israel does not need a king because they are ruled by God the Creator. The great creation hymn, Psalm 104, appears as an integral part of the psalms that conclude the fourth book. Finally, creation pervades the series of hymns that conclude the Psalter.

With a greater emphasis in the fourth and fifth books on the role of God as Creator comes a shift in the understanding of the Creator and of humanity's place in creation. This shift is illustrated by the contrast between Psalm 8 and Psalm 104. Psalm 8 gives humanity a royal role over creation, but Psalm 104 treats humanity as one of many creatures. This continues in Psalms 145–150 where humanity is just one member of the divine choir. Thus, it could be said that the understanding of humanity moves from a position of alienation above creation in the first book to integration into Earth community in books four and five.

As one reads through the Psalter, the way God appears as Creator shifts. One example of this shift appears in different types of the mythic pattern of the storm god. Frank Moore Cross[24] has noticed that there are two types of this pattern: one in which battle is in the foreground and one in which the battle is in the background or has disappeared altogether. The appearance of God as a warrior who does battle on behalf of an individual or nation is common in laments and thanksgiving, but hymns tend to emphasize the second part of the pattern, God's provision of fertility. The astute reader will have noticed that I have shifted from referring to the mythic pattern as the march of the divine warrior, to referring to it as the storm theophany. I have done this to reflect a transformation of the pattern from an emphasis on God as a warrior doing battle in laments to an emphasis on God as storm providing fertility in hymns.

Cooperating with this transformation, the language of God as "maker" of skies and Earth, which seems to presuppose God's creative activity as that of crafting rather than battling, becomes frequent in the fifth and final book of the Psalter. The frequency of God as "maker" reinforces the shift in focus. The image of God shifts from a warrior who appears to deliver an individual or the nation and its king, which is common in the early parts of the Psalter, to a craftsperson who is present in blessing, fertility, and providential care of all creatures.

Along with different images for God, comes a difference in what is expected of God. The psalmist may still wish for deliverance, but gives thanks more frequently, even in the midst of suffering, for God's providential care.

This shift in images for God as Creator is not a simple linear progression but a shift in emphasis. So, psalms with God as Creator present in providential care and blessing appear in the early books of the Psalter, and psalms with God as Creator present as a warrior rescuing people appear occasionally in the fourth and fifth books. Although "the waters of the sea" and "the deeps" (verse 7) are mentioned in Psalm 33, God does not battle them, and creation is by command: "By the word of the LORD, skies were made" (verse 6; author translation). No human king is mentioned, and the psalm has a section that begins—"The LORD brings the counsel of nations to nothing" (verse 10)—that could subvert nation building and governments. Psalm 33 lacks the superscription "Of David," even though it is surrounded by psalms with this superscription. Those who collected and passed down the Psalter may have recognized that this psalm has no connection to monarchy and may even be subversive of the plans of governments. Whatever the case, this is an exception to the general trend in the Psalter and foreshadows later developments in the creation theology of the Psalter. It is an isolated example and does not negate the general trend that has many more examples of the battle against the sea in this section, and many more examples of creation without battle, akin to this psalm, appear later in the Psalter.

Just as there are some psalms in the first three books that do not picture God as a warrior, there are some psalms in books four and five that do picture God as warrior. Psalm 144, a royal lament, praises God who "subdues the peoples under me" (verse 2) and who appears in a storm to battle "aliens" (verse 7).

Make the lightning flash and scatter them;
    send out your arrows and rout them. (144:6)

God is praised as "the one who gives victory to kings, who rescues his servant David" (verse 10). However, it may be significant that the way the psalm ends is with a prayer for healthy children, abundant produce and flocks, and peace (verses 12–15). So it could be said that the way the Creator "rescues" David is not through military victory but through providential care. Therefore, even this appearance of God as a warrior may show evidence of the shift in emphasis because it concludes with a lengthy prayer for God's presence as Creator bringing blessing and fertility. The Creator remains able to intervene as a warrior, but may work in creation for blessing and peace.

Social Order

These different images of the Creator and the creation also authorize different social orders. The imagery of the Creator establishing order as warrior and king can often be seen to legitimize the human king. Or, in other words, God as king and warrior is often linked to royal theology. This is most evident in royal psalms but spills over into other genres. In "royal" psalms, creation theology often serves the interests of the monarchy. I think the designation "royal" is a content, rather than a genre designation, and the royal psalms include several genres. Psalm 18 is a royal psalm in the form of an individual thanksgiving. It contains a lengthy description of a storm theophany (verses 7–16) in which God appears as a warrior to battle the enemies of the king (verse 17). One verse shows the portrayal of God as storm god and warrior:

> And he sent out his arrows, and scattered them;
>> he flashed forth lightnings, and routed them. (verse 14)

The parallelism of arrows and lightnings illustrates the presence of the two metaphors for God—warrior and thunderstorm. The use of these metaphors to legitimate the monarch is then evident when the king says that God "trains my hands for war" (verse 34) followed by a lengthy description of the utter defeat and degradation of his enemies (verses 37–42). A couple of verses are enough to illustrate:

For you girded me with strength for the battle;
>   you made my assailants sink under me (verse 39). . . .
I beat them fine, like dust before the wind;
>   I cast them out like the mire of the streets. (verse 42)

This last verse is similar to a description of the Canaanite goddess Anath's defeat of Death.[25] So the psalm may be describing the human king in language that ancient Near Eastern contemporaries would recognize as mythic. In any case, the imagery of God as storm god and warrior in Psalm 18 clearly legitimates the monarchy and its wars.

Psalm 74, a communal lament, invokes the storm god "who crushed the heads of Leviathan" (verse 14) against national enemies (verses 3–10, 18, 22–23). Psalm 83, another communal lament, names a number of national enemies and prays that God would consume them "as fire consumes the forest" (verse 14) and "so pursue them with your tempest and terrify them with your hurricane" (verse 15).

Although the storm is not in the foreground, the mythic pattern of the defeat of sea is clearly in service of royal theology in Psalm 89. God is portrayed as a warrior defeating sea and a sea monster:

You rule the raging of the sea;
>   when its waves rise, you still them.
You crushed Rahab[26] like a carcass;
>   you scattered your enemies with your mighty arm. (verses
>   9–10)

This mythic pattern clearly legitimates the king as later in the psalm the king is given divine functions. God says:

I will set his hand on the sea
>   and his right hand on the rivers. (verse 25)

In Canaanite Myth, it was the god Baal who defeated a god named Sea and Rivers. In Psalm 89, God gives the king the divine role of defeating the primordial representative of chaos on behalf of God. There is an all too close synergy between God and king here. God fights against the enemies of the king and empowers the king to crush and humiliate his enemies.

Yet, coming as it does at the end the third book, Psalm 89 is a lament for a theology that has failed. The monarchy, and with it this theology, has failed. So this may be an ironic example of the legitimating of the monarchy by the imagery of God as warrior approaching in a storm.

This use of the storm theophany to legitimize the monarchy contrasts with the types of creation theology and implied social order in hymns. The enthronement hymns do not mention a human king and instead emphasize that God is Israel's ruler. The human king has disappeared from view, and God comes not as all powerful warrior, waging war against the peoples, but as Creator and judge who brings justice and equity:

> for he is coming to judge the earth.
> He will judge the world with righteousness,
>   and the peoples with equity. (96:13; author translation)

In Psalm 149, the maintenance of justice has been democratized. It is the faithful, rather than the king, who maintain justice.

The society envisioned by the fifth book could be characterized as priestly. The expression "maker of heaven and earth" appears several times in blessings in the fifth book. The songs of ascent for pilgrims going up to worship in the temple are central to the fifth book. Several psalms refer to priests or other groups gathered for worship in the temple. These psalms and the creation theology presuppose a society centered in the temple and its priests. The contrast between the types of creation that predominate in the first three books and the types of creation that predominate in the fourth and fifth books can be characterized as the difference between royal and priestly social orders. As others have noticed, the people of Israel take over the functions of the king, and God alone becomes king. The type of society implied and envisioned shifts from one centered around king, nation, and the military to one centered around priest, temple, and congregation.

Ecological Order

With the movement from a royal to a priestly social order comes a movement toward a different ecological order. Humans move toward integration into creation. This movement is characterized by the difference between Psalm 8 and Psalm 104. Humans have different roles in Psalm 8 and Psalm 104. In Psalm 8, humans have a royal status *above* creation with "dominion" over all other creatures. In Psalm 104, humans have no special role and are dependent like all other creatures on God's provision of food, water, and the spirit. This movement of humans toward integration into creation is reinforced by the enthronement psalms and the concluding doxologies where humans are just one part of the choir of creatures praising the Creator.

Norman Habel and Geraldine Avent have noticed that Psalms 96–97 "subvert the storm-god tradition of Psalm 29."[27] The features they notice are not confined to these three hymns, but are a convenient place to start a discussion of the ecological features of the larger trends within the Psalter that I am attempting to characterize. Commentators have noticed that Psalm 96 repeats several lines from Psalm 29:

Ascribe to the LORD glory [*kavod*] and strength.

Ascribe to the LORD the glory [*kavod*] of[28] his name;

worship the LORD in holy splendor. (Ps 29:1b-2 par. Ps 96:7b-
8a, 9a)

The repetition of "glory" (*kavod*) makes this word important to both psalms and a number of other words and concepts appear in both psalms. Words from the root *khyl*, "shake, dance," appear in Ps 29:8-9, 96:9, and 97:4. *Forests* appear in both Ps 29:9 and Ps 96:12.

Given these literary affinities between the psalms, the differences are all the more striking. The lines quoted above are preceded in Psalm 29 by the line, "Ascribe to the LORD, O heavenly beings" (verse 1), but are preceded in Psalm 96 by the line, "Ascribe to the LORD, O families of the peoples." So Psalm 29 is addressed to heavenly beings and later worshipers in the temple (verse 9),[29] but Psalm 96 is addressed to "families of the peoples" (verse 7) and, in other verses, "all Earth" and various parts of Earth community (verses 1, 9, 11–12).

Psalm 29 has:

The voice of the LORD shakes (*khyl*) the wilderness,

The LORD shakes (*khyl*) the wilderness of Kadesh.

The voice of the LORD causes oaks to shake (*khyl*) and strips
forests (*y'r*) bare

And in the temple all say "Glory! [*kavod*]" (verses 8–9; author
translation)

The word that is translated "shake" in Psalm 29, is sometimes translated "tremble" in Ps 96:9 and Ps 97:4, but could be translated "dance," because the context in Psalms 96 and 97 is one of praise and rejoicing—"Earth sees and dances!" (97:4; author translation). Thus the voice of God in Psalm 29 shakes Earth community, but Earth community responds with dancing and joy to God's reign in Psalms

96 and 97. Moreover, the forests, which were stripped bare in Psalm 29, sing for joy in Psalm 96: "Then shall the trees of the forest sing for joy" (verse 12).

The word *glory* takes on different connotations in Psalm 96 and 97. God's glory in Psalm 29 is the power and majesty exhibited in the thunderstorm; God's glory and the reasons given for praising God in Psalms 96 and 97 are God's righteousness and justice. Earth community rejoices because God will "judge the peoples with equity" (Ps 96:10) and "will govern the world with justice, and peoples with faithfulness" (96:10; author translation). The "skies declare God's justice" (97:6; author translation) and "righteousness and justice are the foundation of [God's] throne" (97:2). As Habel and Avent put it, "Glory is now seen in life-giving righteousness, not in the destructive thunderclouds."[30] The Creator comes not with a show of power but with righteousness and justice.

As a result of these differences, the images of God and Earth community are quite different. Instead of God who thunders in the skies, it is God "who *made* the skies" (Ps 96:5; author translation). Instead of God shaking the earth, "Earth is firmly established, it shall not be moved" (96:10; author translation). Instead of God's glory being a show of power, God "judge[s] the peoples with equity" (96:10). Instead of just heavenly beings and those in the temple worshipping God, "families of the peoples" are called to give glory to God (96:7). Instead of the earth being a silent object, or even silenced,[31] Earth, the sea and everything in it, fields (96:11-12) and "many islands" (97:1; author translation) are called to rejoice and be glad. They are part of the worshipping community. Instead of the forests being stripped bare, "the trees of the forest sing for joy" (96:12). Instead of a show of power, God's glory and foundation of God's reign are righteousness and justice (97:2). Instead of being the object of God's power, now Earth community is called to worship, dances, and testifies to

God's righteousness and justice. God is Creator and Ruler in Psalm 96 and 97 as in Psalm 29, but the understanding of how God works changes dramatically from powerful warrior to craftsperson, judge, and source of life. The image of Earth community goes from silent, battered object to a subject with a voice. Therefore, the image of God and Earth community in Psalm 29 undergoes a social and ecological transformation in Psalms 96 and 97.

As will be evident from the earlier discussion, this is part of a broader transformation occurring in the Psalter. The image of God as warrior does not disappear, but God as Creator becomes more important, and the focus shifts to God as Maker, justice worker, and life giver. Earth community moves from being an object to being subjects with their own callings as cocreators and worshippers. Human beings shift from being above and separate from Earth community to being fellow workers and worshippers in creation. The Psalter is edited for study and mediation, so as readers move through the Psalter, they are lead by the paradigmatic worshipper David through the experience of Israel with God on a journey that is potentially a social and ecological transformation of their understanding of God. This transformation culminates in Pss 145-150 with human beings integrated into all creation's praise of the Creator.

The Song of a River

Does creation's praise make any sense in the modern world? Can this kind of imagery be useful in imagining different scientific and social realities? Some hints may be available from Aldo Leopold's *Sand County Almanac*. Published in 1949, a year after Leopold's death, it has become a classic in nature writing. Leopold was a conservationist who worked for the U.S. government and later as a professor at the University of Wisconsin. In the book, he has an essay about the Rio

Gavilan, a river that runs down out of the Sierra Madre range in the southwestern United States:

> The song of a river ordinarily means the tune that waters play on rock, root, and rapid.
>
> The Rio Gavilan has such a song. It is a pleasant music, bespeaking dancing riffles and fat rainbow laired under mossy roots of sycamore, oak, and pine. . . .
>
> This song of the waters is audible to every ear, but there is other music in these hills, by no means audible to all. To hear even a few notes of it you must first live here for a long time, and you must know the speech of hills and rivers. Then on a still night, when the campfire is low and the Pleiades have climbed over rimrocks, sit quietly and listen for a wolf to howl, and think hard of everything you have seen and tried to understand. Then you may hear it—a vast pulsing harmony—its score inscribed on a thousand hills, its notes the lives and deaths of plants and animals, its rhythms spanning the seconds and the centuries.
>
> The life of every river sings its own song, but in most the song is long since marred by the discords of misuse. Overgrazing first mars the plants and then the soil. Rifle, trap, and poison next deplete the larger birds and mammals; then comes a park or forest with roads and tourists. Parks are made to bring the music to the many, but by the time many are attuned to hear it there is little left but noise. . . .
>
> Food is the continuum in the Song of the Gavilan. I mean, of course, not only your food, but food for the oak which feeds the buck who feeds the cougar who dies under an oak and goes back into acorns for his erstwhile prey. This is one of many food cycles starting from and returning to oaks. . . .
>
> Science contributes moral as well as material blessings to the world. Its great moral contribution is objectivity, or the

scientific point of view. . . . One of the facts hewn to by science is that every river needs more people, and all people need more inventions, and hence more science; the good life depends on the indefinite extension of this chain of logic. That the good life on any river may likewise depend on the perception of its music, and the preservation of some music to perceive, is a form of doubt not yet entertained by science.

Science has not yet arrived on the Gavilan, so the otter plays tag in its pools and riffles and chases the fat rainbows from under its mossy banks with never a thought for the flood that one day will scour the bank into the Pacific, or for the sportsman who will one day dispute his title to the trout. Like the scientist, he has no doubts about his own design for living. He assumes that for him the Gavilan will sing for ever.[32]

I would distinguish science and technology; technology rather than science is the one that identifies the good life with ever more inventions for ever more people. But perhaps this is a distinction that protects science. Fortunately, since Leopold wrote, there has been a growing awareness among scientists that they are not detached observers, that reality is perceived through paradigms, and that new metaphors like the ones the Psalms and Leopold use are necessary to create better scientific paradigms. This metaphor of music may help us imagine realities that have been largely hidden and, if not perceived, may lead to our death as a species. To some this may seem unscientific. However, the worldview traditionally shared by science that sees humanity as separate from a natural world perceived as object is part of the problem that has created the ecological crisis. Scientists now widely recognize that the detached observer is a fiction and are seeking other ways of understanding the role of the scientist. Music is one metaphor that might describe this new understanding. We are a part of the song.

Summary and Conclusions

Therefore, this book has shown that a social and ecologically liberative creation theology is central to the message of the Psalter. The Psalter has been edited to function as instruction on the journey of faith. As a person of faith travels through the Psalter, their understanding of God, humanity, and Earth is transformed.

The five books of the Psalter tell the story of Israel. The first three books tell the story of the reign of David and his descendants down to the exile to Babylon. David serves as a guide to the path of the just person in the first two books and is replaced by priestly singers in the third book and the tumultuous years leading up to the exile. The dominant understanding of God as Creator in these books sees God as king, warrior, and judge who intervenes on behalf of the nation. Books four and five tell the story of the exile and restoration, respectively. David reappears in the fifth book leading the people in worship of the Creator. God is portrayed far more often as Creator and the understanding of God as Creator changes. A battle against enemies is in the background or absent altogether and replaced with an understanding of God working in creation to care for all creatures and provide abundant life.

A reader who follows David and the nation of Israel on this journey of study, meditation, prayer, and praise, has their understanding of God, humanity, and Earth transformed. The image of God shifts from the God of a nation to God as Creator present in and for all creation. Humanity goes from lament, alienation, and separation from creation to being integrated into all creation's praise of the Creator. Earth community goes from being silent objects of domination to living subjects who raise their voices in praise and joy.

This creation theology is ecological because the Creator is present in creation as the spirit of life and source of fertility. Earth community responds to the Creator with praise and joy. Earth is alive and has a voice with which it responds to the Creator with joy and praise. Humanity and human worship is integrated into all creation's praise of the Creator.

The book has proposed several methodological innovations. It has shown that genre criticism could profitably be expanded by the inclusion of narrative elements in the descriptions of genres. This analysis of recurring stories is important to appreciate what is unique, understand the story world of the text, and analyze the contemporary power of biblical narratives as they interact with contemporary stories. In this regard, the book has also advocated the need for a critical method that begins to understand and analyze the contemporary social and political power of the Bible. As a tentative step in this direction, I have included some examples of the way biblical images and plots may inform and be informed by contemporary stories and function as symbolic reflections on society and ecology.

The method and content of this study suggests several areas for further research. The description of narrative elements in wisdom psalms, laments, and hymns could be refined and extended to other genres in the Psalter and other biblical books. This would open up numerous connections to contemporary cultural criticism. Biblical studies has focused tremendous energy understanding what the Bible meant in the ancient world but much work remains to be done in gaining a similar depth of understanding of the meanings and functions of the Bible in contemporary society. I hope that the methodological innovations of this work may help biblical studies develop critical methods for understanding the contemporary social function and power of the Bible and that an appreciation of the creation theology of the Psalter may provide resources for church and society to address the political and ecological issues of globalization and imagine a more sustainable and equitable world.

NOTES

Introduction

1. Lynn White Jr., "The Historical Roots of Our Ecological Crisis," *Science* 155 (1967): 1205.
2. *An Inconvenient Truth*, directed by David Guggenheim (Paramount, 2006).
3. *Keeping the Earth: Religious and Scientific Perspectives on the Environment* (Cambridge, Mass.: Union of Concerned Scientists, 1996).
4. Brevard S. Childs, *Introduction to the Old Testament as Scripture* (Philadelphia: Fortress Press, 1979), 508.
5. White, "The Historical Roots," 1205.
6. Ibid., 1207.
7. I have not corrected White's exclusive language. He frequently uses "man" and male pronouns for humanity.
8. White, "The Historical Roots," 1205.
9. Ibid., 1205.
10. Ibid., 1205.
11. Val Plumwood, *Feminism and the Mastery of Nature* (New York: Routledge, 1993), 43, quoted in Norman Habel, ed., *Readings from the Perspective of Earth*, The Earth Bible, vol. 1 (Sheffield, England: Sheffield Academic, 2000), 40–41.
12. Anne Primavesi, *From Apocalypse to Genesis: Ecology, Feminism and Christianity* (Minneapolis: Fortress Press, 1991), ix.

13. Heather Eaton, *Introducing Ecofeminist Theologies*, Introducing Feminist Theologies 12 (London: T & T Clark International, 2005), 73.

14. Norman Habel, "Introducing the Earth Bible," in Habel, *Readings*, 31.

15. Habel, *Readings*, 24, 42–53.

16. "Psalm 104: A Celebration of the *Vanua*," in *The Earth Story in the Psalms and the Prophets*, The Earth Bible, vol. 4, ed. Norman Habel (Sheffield, England: Sheffield Academic, 2001), 84–97.

17. Sallie McFague, "An Earthly Theological Agenda," in *Ecofeminism and the Sacred*, ed. Carol J. Adams (New York: Continuum, 1993), 90.

18. Sallie McFague, *The Body of God: An Ecological Theology* (Minneapolis: Fortress Press, 1993); *Life Abundant: Rethinking Theology and Economy for a Planet in Peril* (Minneapolis: Fortress Press, 2001); *Models of God: Theology for an Ecological, Nuclear Age* (Philadelphia: Fortress Press, 1987); *Supernatural Christians: How We Should Love Nature* (Minneapolis: Fortress Press, 1997).

19. Northrop Frye, *Anatomy of Criticism: Four Essays* (Princeton, N.J.: Princeton University Press, 1957).

20. Northrop Frye, *The Great Code: The Bible and Literature* (San Diego, New York, and London: Harcourt, 1982); *Words with Power: Being a Second Study of "The Bible and Literature"* (New York: Viking, Penguin Books, 1990).

21. James M. Kee and Adele Reinhartz, eds., *Northrop Frye and the Afterlife of the Word* (Semeia, vol. 89; Atlanta: The Society of Biblical Literature, 2002). Even in this volume that sought to rectify the situation, most of the articles are by English professors.

22. Fredric Jameson, *The Political Unconscious: Narrative as Socially Symbolic Act* (Ithaca, N.Y.: Cornell University Press, 1981), 69–70.

23. Laurence Coupe, *Myth*, The New Critical Idiom, ed. John Drakakis (London: Routledge, 1997), 159–73.

24. Frye's insight into the social importance of story comes from his reading of Giovanni Battista Vico (1668–1744). See Frye, *Words with Power*, 82; Gimabattista Vico, *New Science: Principles of the New Science Concerning the Common Nature of Nations*, trans. David Marsh (London: Penguin Books, 2001).

25. These are the most widely used names for the genres. Both the names *lament* and *thanksgiving* may impose modern ideas on the

genres. Some scholars note that laments could more accurately be called complaints or petitions, because they typically complain to God about some situation and ask God to act. Claus Westermann notes that Hebrew does not have a concept corresponding to our "thanks" and prefers to call *thanksgiving*, which praises God for a specific act, *declarative praise*, and the hymn, which praises God's character and behavior generally, *descriptive praise*, in order to indicate that they are both praise of God. Claus Westermann, *Praise and Lament in the Psalms*, trans. Keith R. Crim and Richard N. Soulen (Atlanta: John Knox, 1981), 25–35.

26. James Muilenburg, "Form Criticism and Beyond," *JBL* 88 (1969): 1–18.

27. Brevard S. Childs, *Biblical Theology in Crisis* (Philadelphia: Westminster, 1970). In subsequent books, he worked out the canonical interpretation of the Bible as the canon of Christian scripture.

28. Childs, *Introduction*, 508–511.

29. This may make the questionable assumption, dubbed the "intentional fallacy," that the intentions of the compilers determine contemporary meaning. William K. Wimsatt and Monroe C. Beardsley, "The Intentional Fallacy," *Sewanee Review* 54 (1946): 468–488.

Revised and republished in William K. Wimsatt, *The Verbal Icon: Studies in the Meaning of Poetry* (Lexington: University of Kentucky Press, 1954): 3–18.

30. Nancy L. deClaissé-Walford, *Introduction to the Psalms: A Song from Ancient Israel* (St. Louis: Chalice, 2004), 129.

31. Ibid.

32. Renita Weems, *Battered Love: Marriage, Sex, and Violence in the Hebrew Prophets*, Overtures to Biblical Theology (Minneapolis: Fortress Press, 1995).

33. William P. Brown, *Seeing the Psalms: A Theology of Metaphor* (Louisville, Ky.: Westminster John Knox, 2002).

34. J. Richard Middleton, "Is Creation Theology Inherently Conservative: A Dialogue with Walter Brueggemann," *HTR* 87 (1994): 257–77; Walter Brueggemann, "Response to J. Richard Middleton," *HTR* 87 (1994): 279–89.

35. Habel, *Readings*, 28–29.

Chapter One: "Like a Tree Planted"

1. Ps 1:3, author translation.
2. Gerald H. Wilson, *The Editing of the Hebrew Psalter,* SBLDS 76 (Chico, Calif.: Scholars, 1985), 173–81, 204; See, by way of comparison, also Gerald H. Wilson, "The Use of Untitled Psalms in the Hebrew Psalter," *ZAW* 97 (1985): 404–13.
3. Gerald H. Wilson, "The Shape of the Book of Psalms," *Int* 46 (192): 134; See also by the same author "Shaping the Psalter: A Consideration of Editorial Linkage in the Book of Psalms" in *Shape and Shaping of the Psalter,* ed. J. Clinton McCann (Sheffield, England: JSOT, 1993), 72–82.
4. Claus Westermann, *Praise and Lament in the Psalms,* trans. Keith R. Crim and Richard N. Soulen (Atlanta: John Knox, 1981), 252–53.
5. Wilson, *Editing of the Hebrew Psalter,* 222–23.
6. James L. Mays, "The Place of the Torah-Psalms," *JBL* 106, no. 1 (1987): 3–12.
7. Hermann Gunkel and Joachim Begrich, *Introduction to Psalms: The Genres of the Religious Lyric of Israel,* trans. James D. Nogalski (Macon, Ga.: Mercer University Press, 1998), 295–97; Erhard S. Gerstenberger, *Psalms: Part 1 with an Introduction to Cultic Poetry,* vol. 14 of The Forms of Old Testament Literature, ed. Rolf Knierim and Gene M. Tucker (Grand Rapids, Mich.: Eerdmans, 1988), 19–21.
8. Gunkel and Begrich, *Introduction to Psalms,* 303; Gerstenberger, *Psalms: Part 1,* 19.
9. Gerstenberger, *Psalms: Part 1,* 21.
10. J. Clinton McCann Jr., *A Theological Introduction to the Book of Psalms: The Psalms as Torah* (Nashville: Abingdon, 1993), 26.
11. William P. Brown, *Seeing the Psalms: A Theology of Metaphor* (Louisville, Ky.: Westminster John Knox, 2002), 57, 89–100.
12. William G. Braude, *The Midrash on Psalms,* Yale Judaica Series 13 (New Haven, Conn.: Yale University Press, 1954), 1:5.
13. Wilson, *Editing of the Hebrew Psalter,* 139–97.
14. McCann, *A Theological Introduction,* 27.
15. Walter Brueggemann, "Bounded by Obedience and Praise: The Psalms as Canon," *JSOT* 50 (1991): 63–92.
16. Brown, *Seeing the Psalms,* 56–57.
17. Psalms 1:1, 6; 36:5; 37:5, 7, 14, 23, 34; 49:14; 91:11; 119:1, 3, 5, 14, 26, 29, 32, 35, 37, 59, 168; 128:1.

18. Brown, *Seeing the Psalms*, 60–74.

19. Ibid., 63–67.

20. Othmar Keel, *Goddesses and Trees, New Moon and Yahweh: Ancient Near Eastern Art and the Hebrew Bible*, JSOTSup 61 (Sheffield, England: Sheffield Academic, 1998), 48.

21. Dexter E. Callender Jr., *Adam in Myth and History: Ancient Israelite Perspectives on the Primal Human*, HSS 48 (Winona Lake, Ind.: Eisenbrauns, 2000), 50–54.

22. Brown, *Seeing the Psalms*, 63, citing E. O. James, *The Tree of Life: An Archaeological Study* (Studies in the History of Religions, XI; Leiden: Brill, 1966), 37–38 and Elizabeth Bloch-Smith, "'Who is the King of Glory?': Solomon's Temple and Its Symbolism," in *Scripture and Other Artifacts: Essays on the Bible and Archaeology in Honor of Philip J. King*, ed. M.D. Coogan, J. C. Exum, L. E. Stager (Louisville, Ky.: Westminster John Knox, 1994), 23.

23. Brown, *Seeing the Psalms*, 78.

24. Ibid., 15–53.

25. Psalm 36:6.

26. Walter Zimmerli, "The Place and Limit of Wisdom in the Framework of Old Testament Theology," *SJT* 17 (1964): 148.

27. Norman Habel, ed., *Readings from the Perspective of Earth*, The Earth Bible, vol. 1 (Sheffield, England: Sheffield Academic, 2000), 28–29.

28. Othmar Keel, *The Symbolism of the Biblical World: Ancient Near Eastern Iconography and the Book of Psalms*, trans. Timothy J. Hallett. (New York: Seabury, 1978), 190–92.

Chapter Two: "God My Rock"

1. Psalm 42:9.

2. *The Lion King*, directed by Roger Allers and Rob Minkoff (Disney, 1994).

3. Brevard S. Childs, *Introduction to the Old Testament as Scripture* (Philadelphia: Fortress Press, 1979), 521–22; Gerald H. Wilson, *The Editing of the Hebrew Psalter*, SBLDS 76 (Chico, Calif.: Scholars, 1985), 172–73.

4. This list of elements is based on Westermann's description and informed by the works of Gunkel and Begrich, and Gerstenberger. Claus Westermann, *Praise and Lament in the Psalms*, trans. Keith R.

Crim and Richard N. Soulen (Atlanta: John Knox, 1981), 64–78; Hermann Gunkel and Joachim Begrich, *Introduction to Psalms: The Genres of the Religious Lyric of Israel*, trans. James D. Nogalski (Macon, Ga.: Mercer University Press, 1998), 152–86 (Originally published as *Einleitung in die Psalmen: die Gattungen der religiösen Lyrik Israels*, Göttinger Hankommentar zum Alten Testament (Göttingen: Vandenhoeck & Ruprecht, 1933); Erhard S. Gerstenberger, *Psalms: Part 1 with an Introduction to Cultic Poetry*, The Forms of Old Testament Literature, vol. 14, ed. Rolf Knierim and Gene M. Tucker (Grand Rapids, Mich.: Eerdmans, 1988), 11–14.

5. Psalms 3, 4, 5, 6, 7, 10, 13, 17, 22, 25, 26, 27, 28, 31, 35, 38, 39, 40, 42, 43, 51, 54, 55, 56, 57, 59, 61, 64, 69, 70, 71, 86, 88, 94, 102, 109, 120, 130, 129, 140, 141, 142, 143.

6. Westermann makes a distinction between the *confession of trust*, which comes after the complaint, and the *assurance of being heard*, which comes after the petition. He acknowledges, however, that "confession of trust, certainty of being heard, and praise of God cannot be clearly distinguished" (Westermann, *Praise and Lament*, 70, 74). I have, therefore, included both under the heading of *confession of trust*.

7. Gunkel and Begrich, *Introduction to the Psalms*, 125–26.

8. Joachim Begrich, "Das priesterliche Heilsorakel," *ZAW* 52 (1934), 43.

9. Westermann, *Praise and Lament*, 65, 70.

10. Ibid., 52 n. 1, 64, 69 (table).

11. Ibid., 53–54 (table), 55–57, calls them "motifs." Miller's "motivation clauses" is a more accurate description of their function and content. Patrick D. Miller Jr., *They Cried to the Lord: The Form and Theology of Biblical Prayer* (Minneapolis: Fortress Press, 1994), 57, citing Moshe Greenberg, *Biblical Prose Prayer as a Window to the Popular Religion of Ancient Israel* (Berkeley: University of California Press, 1983), 17, who refers to the "motivating sentence" and Anneli Aejmelaeus, *Traditional Prayer in the Psalms* (BZAW 167; Berlin: Walter de Gruyter, 1986), 88, who has "motivation clause."

12. Westermann, *Praise and Lament*, 189.

13. Ibid.

14. Ibid.

15. Ibid., 189–90.
16. Ibid., 190, quoting Pss 28:3; 41:6; 52:2-4; 55:21; 62:4.
17. Westermann, *Praise and Lament*, 190, quoting Pss 14:1-3 (=53:1, 3-4); 26:10; 28:4; 36:4; 52:1; 55:10, 11, 15; 73:6; 109:17, and so on.
18. Westermann, *Praise and Lament*, 190, citing Pss 5:10; 10:3; 14:1, 4; 28:5; 36:1; 52:7; 54:3; 55:19; 73:27; 86:14; 119:85, 139.
19. Westermann, *Praise and Lament*, 191.
20. Ibid.
21. Ibid., 190.
22. Ibid., 192.
23. See Pss 7:2; 10:9.
24. Three different Hebrew words are translated "lion" in English. The most common in individual laments is 'aryeh. In other genres kphir appears more frequently, and shakhal appears once.
25. Leviathan also appears in Psalm 104:26, but the portrayal of Leviathan, which will be discussed in chap. 5, is either part of a different tradition, or the mythic pattern has been transformed.
26. Frank Moore Cross, *Canaanite Myth and Hebrew Epic: Essays in the History of the Religion of Israel* (Cambridge, Mass.: Harvard University Press, 1973).
27. Cross, *Canaanite Myth*, 162–63. See also Patrick D. Miller Jr., *The Divine Warrior in Early Israel*, HSM, vol. 5 (Cambridge, Mass.: Harvard University Press, 1973); Arthur Walker-Jones, "Alternative Cosmogonies in the Psalms" (Ph.D. diss., Princeton Theological Seminary, 1991), 65–66.
28. Jörg Jeremias, *Theophanie: Die Geschichte enier alttestamentlichen Gattung*, Wissenschaftliche Monographien zum Alten und Neuen Testament 10, 2d ed. (Neukirchen-Vluyn, 1977).
29. George Molin, "Das Motiv vom Chaoskampf im Alten Orient und in den Traditionen Jerusalems und Israels," in *Memoria Jerusalem; Freundesgabe Franz Sauer zum 70. Geburtstag* (Graz, Austria: Akademische Druck- u. Verlagsanstalt, 1977), 13–28.
30. Psalms 69:3, 15; 130:1.
31. Mary K. Wakeman has argued that "Earth" is another name for Death in the Hebrew Bible, and, therefore, the battle against Mot is present in several biblical passages, but others, like John Day have

not been convinced. Mary K. Wakeman, "The Biblical Earth Monster in Cosmogonic Myth," *JBL* 88 (1969): 313–20; Mary K. Wakeman, *God's Battle with the Monster: A Study in Biblical Imagery* (Leiden: E. J. Brill, 1973), 106–17; John Day, *God's Conflict with the Dragon and the Sea* (Cambridge: Cambridge University Press, 1985), 84.

32. Michael David Coogan, ed., *Stories from Ancient Canaan* (Louisville, Ky.: Westminster, 1978), 106.

33. Ibid., 107.

34. See also Ps 40:2, an individual thanksgiving, "He drew me up from the desolate pit, out of the miry bog, and set my feet upon a rock, making my steps secure."

35. Karin Lesnik-Oberstein, "Children's Literature and the Environment," in *Writing the Environment: Ecocriticism & Literature*, ed. Richard Kerridge and Neil Sammells (London and New York: Zed, 1998), 216.

36. Jean-Jacques Rousseau, *Emile*, trans. by Barbara Foxley (London: Dent // New York: Dutton, 1911), 76, 84, 147–148, cited in Lesnik-Oberstein, "Children's Literature," 211.

37. Lesnik-Oberstein, "Children's Literature," 208.

38. J. R. R. Tolkien, *The Lord of the Rings* (Boston: Houghton & Mifflin, 1993).

39. *The Lord of the Rings: The Two Towers*, directed by Peter Jackson (Miramar, 2002).

40. Mary Daly, *Beyond God the Father: Toward a Philosophy of Women's Liberation* (Boston: Beacon, 1973), 19.

41. This might seem to contradict my statement in the previous chapter that the use of the tree as a metaphor for the just person had ecological potential because it blurred boundaries between divinity, humanity, and Earth, but it is a divine humanity separated from Earth that is the problem here.

42. Psalms 18:2 (two times), 31, 46; 19:14; 28:1; 31:2, 3; 42:9; 62:2, 6, 7; 71:3 (two times); 78:35; 89:26; 92:15; 94:22; 95:1; 144:1, 2.

43. Psalms 68:5; 89:26; 103:13. (Perhaps Ps 27:10 could also be included.)

Chapter Three: Making Peace with Leviathan

1. This list of elements is based on Westermann's description, and informed by the works of Gunkel and Begrich, and Gerstenberger.

Claus Westermann, *Praise and Lament in the Psalms*, trans. Keith R. Crim and Richard N. Soulen (Atlanta: John Knox, 1981), 52–44; Hermann Gunkel and Joachim Begrich, *Introduction to Psalms: The Genres of the Religious Lyric of Israel*, trans. James D. Nogalski (Macon, Ga.: Mercer University Press, 1998), 85–97; Erhard S. Gerstenberger, *Psalms: Part 1 with an Introduction to Cultic Poetry*, The Forms of Old Testament Literature, col. 14, ed. Rolf Knierim and Gene M. Tucker (Grand Rapids, Mich.: Eerdmans, 1988), 11–14.

2. See chap. 2, n. 11.

3. Northrop Frye, *Anatomy of Criticism: Four Essays* (Princeton, N.J.: Princeton University Press, 1957), 43, 99–100, 143–44, 152–53.

4. Westermann, *Praise and Lament*, 59.

5. Ibid., 61.

6. Ibid., 64.

7. Ibid., *Praise and Lament*, 55–57.

8. For clarity I have used the NRSV's translation "rebuke," but "roar" or "shout" would be a better translation. P. Joüon, "Notes de Lexicography Hebraique," *Bib* 6 (1925): 318–21; A. A. Macintosh, "A Consideration of Hebrew g'r," *VT* 19 (1969): 471–79; S. C. Reif, "A Note on g'r," *VT* 21 (1971), 241–44.

9. Psalms 18:15; 104:6–7; Job 26:11; Isa 17:13; 50:2; Nah.1:4.

10. *KTU* 1.2 I 24.

11. Herman Melville, *Moby Dick* (Hertfordshire: Wordsworth Classics, 1993); *Free Willy*, directed by Simon Wincer (Warner Brothers Pictures, 1993).

12. Frye, *Anatomy of Criticism*, 100, 155; Northrop Frye, *Words with Power: Being a Second Study of "The Bible as Literature"* (London: Penguin, 1990), 234, 284–285.

13. Melville, *Moby Dick*, 341–42.

14. Ibid., 68.

15. Thomas B. Lawrence and Nelson Phillips, "From *Moby Dick* to *Free Willy*: Macro-Cultural Discourse and Institutional Entrepreneurship in Emerging Institutional Fields," *Organization* 11 (2004): 689–711.

16. Ibid., 695–97.

17. Ibid., 697–98.

18. *Whale Rider*, directed by Niki Caro (ApolloMedia, 2004).

Chapter Four: "The LORD, Maker of Heaven and Earth"

1. Arvid Kapelrud, "Creation in the Ras Shamra Texts," *ST* 34 (1980): 3.
2. Dennis J. McCarthy, "'Creation' Motifs in Ancient Hebrew Poetry," in *Creation in the Old Testament*, ed. Bernhard Anderson (Philadelphia: Fortress Press, 1984), 85, n. 1.
3. John Gray, *The Biblical Doctrine of the Reign of God* (Edinburgh: T. & T. Clark, 1979), 19.
4. M. Dietrich, O. Loretz, and J. Sanmartin, eds., *The Cuneiform Alphabetic Texts from Ugarit, Ras Ibn Hani, and Other Places* (Münster: Ugarit-Verlag, 1995), 1.5 VI 23–24; 1.6 I 6–7, II 17–19, IV 24–29. (*CTU*)
5. *CTU*, 1.6 III 6–7, 12–13.
6. R. J. Clifford, "Cosmogonies in the Ugaritic Texts and in the Bible," *Orientalia* n.s. 53 (1984): 186–87.
7. Arthur Walker-Jones, "Alternative Cosmogonies in the Psalms" (Ph.D. diss., Princeton Theological Seminary, 1991), 49.
8. Ben C. Ollenburger, "Isaiah's Creation Theology," *Ex Auditu* 3 (1987): 60.
9. Claus Westermann, *Genesis 1–11: A Commentary* (Minneapolis: Augsburg Publishing House, 1984), 175.
10. See, by way of comparison, Psalm 128; Kent Harold Richards, "Bless/Blessing" in *The Anchor Bible Dictionary*, vol. 1, ed. David Noel Freedman (New York: Doubleday, 1992), 754; Josef Scharbert, "*brk*," in *Theological Dictionary of the Old Testament*, vol. 2, ed. G. Johannes Botterweck and Helmer Ringgren, trans. John T. Willis (Grand Rapids: Mich.: Eerdmans, 1977), 288, 294, 303. Recent studies also emphasize that *blessing* has to do with strengthening relationships between individuals and groups.
11. Terence E. Fretheim, *God and World in the Old Testament: A Relational Theology of Creation* (Nashville: Abingdon, 2005), 10–13, 157–98.
12. Robin W. Lovin and Frank E. Reynolds, eds., *Cosmology and Ethical Order: New Studies in Comparative Ethics* (Chicago: The University of Chicago Press, 1985), 5.
13. Lovin and Reynolds, *Cosmology*, 18–19.
14. William P. Brown, *The Ethos of the Cosmos: The Genesis of Moral Imagination in the Bible* (Grand Rapids, Mich.: Eerdmans, 1999), 33.

15. Ronald A. Simkins, *Creator and Creation: Nature in the Worldview of Ancient Israel* (Peabody, Mass.: Hendrickson, 1994); William P. Brown, *Seeing the Psalms: A Theology of Metaphor* (Louisville, Ky.: Westminster John Knox, 2002), 105–34, 155–66; Fretheim, *God and World*, 1–3.

16. Frank Moore Cross, *Canaanite Myth and Hebrew Epic: Essays in the History of the Religion of Israel* (Cambridge, Mass.: Harvard University Press, 1973), 162.

17. Claus Westermann, *Praise and Lament in the Psalms*, trans. Keith R. Crim and Richard N. Soulen (Atlanta: John Knox, 1981), 155.

18. Ibid., 257.

19. Nancy deClaissé-Walford, *Introduction to the Psalms* (St. Louis: Chalice, 2004), 42.

20. Westermann, *Praise and Lament*, 32.

21. deClaissé-Walford, *Introduction*, 99.

22. Gerald H. Wilson, "The Use of Royal Psalms at the 'Seams' of the Hebrew Psalter," *JSOT* 35 (1986): 92; quoted in J. Clinton McCann Jr., *A Theological Introduction to the Book of Psalms: The Psalms as Torah.* (Nashville: Abingdon, 1993), 662; see also James L. Mays, *The Lord Reigns: A Theological Handbook to the Psalms* (Louisville, Ky.: Westminster John Knox, 1994), 12–22.

23. "The Creation Epic," trans. E. A. Speiser, and "The Creation Epic—Additions to Tablets V–VII," trans. A. K. Grayson, in James B. Pritchard, ed. *Ancient Near Eastern Texts Relating to the Old Testament,* 3d ed. (Princeton, N.J.: Princeton University Press, 1969), 501–3; Thorkild Jacobsen, *The Treasures of Darkness: A History of Mesopotamian Religion* (New Haven and London: Yale University Press, 1976), 167–91.

24. H. W. F. Saggs, *The Encounter with the Divine in Mesopotamia and Israel*, Jordan Lectures 1976 (London: Athlone, 1978), 58–59.

25. Psalms 103:1, 2, 22; 104:1, 35.

26. The word "works" is in each case the Hebrew noun *ma'aseh*.

27. Patrick D. Miller Jr., "The Poetry of Creation: Psalm 104" in *God Who Creates: Essays in Honour of W. Sibley Towner*, ed. William P. Brown and S. Dean McBride Jr. (Grand Rapids, Mich.: Eerdmans, 2000), 102.

28. Psalms 104:35; 105:45; 106:1, 48; 111:1; 112:1; 113:1, 9; 115:18; 116:19; 117:2; 135:1, 21; 146:1, 10; 147:1, 20; 148:1, 14; 149:1, 9; 150:1, 6.
29. Psalms 74:16; 93:1-2.
30. Miller, "Poetry," 102.
31. Fretheim, *God and World* 109–26; Terence E. Fretheim, "The Plagues as Ecological Signs of Historical Disaster," *JBL* 110 (1991): 385–96; Terrence E. Fretheim, *Exodus* (Louisville, Ky.: John Knox, 1991), 13.
32. The description recalls Death swallowing Baal. Mary K. Wakeman, "The Biblical Earth Monster in Cosmogonic Myth," *JBL* 88 (1969): 313–20; Mary K. Wakeman, *God's Battle with the Monster: A Study in Biblical Imagery* (Leiden: E. J. Brill, 1973), 106–17.
33. The Hebrew (MT) has "flaming fire," which is feminine singular in Hebrew, but "ministers" is masculine plural. Thus NRSV and others read "fire and flame" to match "ministers."
34. The Hebrew word *'sh*, "fire," and different forms of the root *lht*, "flame," are used in both Ps 104:4 and Ps 106:18.
35. Gerald Henry Wilson, *The Editing of the Hebrew Psalter*, SBLDS 76 (Chico, Calif.: Scholars, 1985), 173–81, 204; see, by way of comparison, also "The Use of Untitled Psalms in the Hebrew Psalter," *ZAW* 97 (1985): 404–13.
36. The Hebrew can be translated either "heavens" or "skies," and I tend to prefer "skies" in order to overcome the idea of heaven as "some distant celestial place" and the resultant dualism between heaven and Earth. Norman Habel, "Geophany: The Earth Story in Genesis 1," in *The Earth Story in Genesis*, ed. Norman C. Habel and Shirley Wurst (Earth Bible, vol. 2; Sheffield: Sheffield Academic Press // Cleveland, Ohio: Pilgrim, 2000), 41.
37. Psalms 113:1, 9; 115:18; 116:19; 117:1, 2. Unlike the others in this list that have the short form of the name of God, Ps 117:1 has the long form.
38. Erhard Gerstenberger, *Psalms Part 2 and Lamentations*, The Forms of the Old Testament Literature, vol. 15 (Grand Rapids, Mich.: Eerdmans, 2001), 283.
39. Gerstenberger, *Psalms*, 289–90.
40. I have modified the NRSV translation, which has "the earth" in order to treat Earth as a subject.

41. Fretheim, *God and World*, 255.

42. Ibid., 266–67.

43. Job 38:7; Pss 19:1-2; 50:6; 65:8, 12-13; 69:34; 89:5, 12; 93:3; 96:11-2; 97:6; 98:7-8; 99:1; 103:22; 145:10-11; 148:4, 7-10; 150:6; Isa 35:1-2; 42:10-12; 43:20; 44:23; 49:13; 55:12; 66:23; Jer 51:48; Joel 2:21; Hab 3:3.

44. *WALL·E*, directed by Andrew Stanton (Pixar, 2008).

45. Eve is an acronym for "Extra-terrestrial Vegetation Evaluator."

Chapter Five: "Food to the Hungry"

1. Walter Brueggemann, *Israel's Praise: Doxology against Idolatry and Ideology* (Philadelphia: Fortress Press, 1988), 101.

2. Ibid., 90.

3. Ibid., 101.

4. Ibid., 102.

5. Ibid., 101, n. 21.

6. Ibid., 101.

7. Ibid.

8. J. Richard Middleton, "Is Creation Theology Inherently Conservative: A Dialogue with Walter Brueggemann," *HTR* 87 (1994): 257–77; Walter Brueggemann, "Response to J. Richard Middleton," *HTR* 87 (1994): 279–89.

9. Middleton, "Is Creation Theology," 277.

10. Ibid., 264.

11. Emil Brunner, "Nature and Grace," in *Natural Theology*, Emil Brunner and Karl Barth, trans. Peter Frankel (London: G. Bles, 1946), 51.

12. Middleton, "Is Creation Theology," 273, citing Pedro Trigo, *Creation and History* (Maryknoll, N.Y.: Orbis, 1991), 69–108.

13. Terence E. Fretheim, "The Plagues as Ecological Signs of Historical Disaster," *JBL* 110 (1991): 363; Terence Fretheim, "The Reclamation of Creation: Redemption and Law in Exodus," *Int* 45 (1991): 358–64. Fretheim has repeated these arguments recently in *God and World in the Old Testament: A Relational Theology of Creation* (Nashville: Abingdon, 2005), 109–31.

14. Middleton, "Is Creation Theology," 267, citing J. Richard Middleton, "The Liberating Image? Interpreting the *Imago Dei* in Context," *Christian Scholar's Review* 24 (1994): 6–23.
15. This example is from Cornel West in a class I took with him when I was a student.
16. I would take the reference to the "pillar of cloud" (verse 7) as a historical example of the appearance of God in a storm, and the call for the earth to "quake" (verse 1) and the reference to worship on God's "holy mountain" (verse 9) as evidence of the narrative pattern of the myth.
17. H. L. Ginsberg, trans., "Poems about Baal and Anat," in James B. Pritchard, ed., *Ancient Near Eastern Texts Relating to the Old Testament* (3d ed.; Princeton: Princeton University Press, 1969), 131.
18. An indication that the "kingship" of God is in view, not the disastrous kingship of human kings, may be evident in the choice of verbs (Ps 96:13). The verb used for God's good governance is not the verb from the same root as *king*, but the root that refers back to Israel's charismatic leaders before the rise of kingship. The noun and the verb from this root are the ones commonly translated "judge." But this translation of the word is misleading in English. An examination of what the so-called judges do in the book of Judges reveals an identity and much wider variety of functions than our modern concept of a judge. They are people called and empowered by God to provide different types of leadership for different crisis situations. They function as priests, prophets, leaders, and warriors. Perhaps, this type of spirit-filled, situational leadership is a better metaphor for God's leadership.
19. Thomas Krüger, "'Kosmo-theologie' zwischen Mythos und Erfahrung: Psalm 104 im Horizon altorientalischer und alttestamentlicher 'Schöpfungs'-Konzepte." *BN* 68 (1993): 71, cited in Karl Löning and Erich Zenger, *To Begin with, God Created*, trans. Omar Kaste (Collegeville, Minn.: Michael Glazier, 2000), 35.
20. Löning and Zenger, *To Begin with*," 34.
21. James C. Scott, *Domination and the Arts of Resistance: Hidden Transcripts* (New Haven, Conn.: Yale University Press, 1990).
22. Jon D. Levenson, *Creation and the Persistence of Evil: The Jewish Drama of Divine Omnipotence* (Princeton, N.J.: Princeton University Press, 1994), 17, citing a student. Levenson himself thinks the imagery is

of God using Leviathan *for sport* as a fisherman (Job 40:25-26) and connects the image with the setting of boundaries for the waters (Ps 104:6-9).

23. Ending a hymn with a petition is unique, but not without precedent. In any case, the mixing and overlap of genres is part of their nature so that the use of unique elements in a genre is to be expected, not denied.

24. Brueggemann, *Israel's Praise*, 90.

25. Fredric Jameson, "A Conversation with Fredric Jameson," *Semeia* 59 (1992): 228–29.

26. I have modified the NRSV translation, which has "the earth," in order to treat Earth as a subject.

27. Once again, I have modified the NRSV translation, which has "the earth," in order to treat Earth as a subject.

28. The Qere, the Cairo Geniza, and many Targums have the plural *words*. The Kethib and a number of versions have the singular *word*. Whether the word is singular or plural, it is the same Hebrew word as in verse 18, and I have italicized to emphasize the parallelism.

29. Here and in the following verse I have modified the NRSV by replacing "ordinances" with "judgments" to indicate that this Hebrew word has to do with judgments in a court of law and therefore justice.

30. Exodus 15:25; Lev 26:46; Deut 4:1, 5, 8, 14, 45; 5:1, 31; 6:1, 20; 7:11; 11:32; 12:1; 26:16-17; Josh 24:25; 1 Sam 30:25; 1 Kgs 8:58; 9:4; 2 Kgs 17:37; 1 Chr 22:13; 2 Chr 7:17; 19:10; 33:8; Ezra 7:10; Neh 1:7; 9:13; 10:30; Ps 81:5; 147:19; Ezek 11:12; 20:18, 25; 36:27; Mal 3:22.

31. The translation of this line is from J. Clinton McCann, "The Book of Psalms," in vol. IV of *The New Interpreter's Bible,* ed. Leander Keck, et al. (Nashville: Abingdon, 1996), 1276.

32. Rowland E. Prothero, *The Psalms in Human Life and Experience* (New York: E. P. Dutton, 1903), 115, cited in McCann, "The Book of Psalms," 1276.

33. McCann, "The Book of Psalms," 1276–77.

Chapter Six: "Let Earth Rejoice"

1. Norman Habel, "Introducing the Earth Bible," in *Readings from the Perspective of Earth*, The Earth Bible, vol. 1, ed. Norman Habel (Sheffield: Sheffield Academic, 2000), 28.

2. The Hebrew word translated as "tides" here is frequently translated "river." In Ugaritic myth, Baal battles a god who's name is both Sea and River (*ANET*, 131). The two words occur frequently in parallel in similar contexts in the Hebrew Bible. It makes sense to me to think of the word as referring to the currents created by tides as rivers in the sea. The translation "tides" makes sense in this context because here, as elsewhere, their voice is related to the sea in the next verse.

3. Arthur Walker-Jones, "Honey from the Rock: The Contribution of God as Rock to an Ecological Hermeneutic," in *Exploring Ecological Hermeneutics*, eds. Norman Habel and Peter Trudinger (Atlanta: Society of Biblical Literature, 2008), 97.

4. Exodus 17:1-7.

5. The Hebrew word that I have translated as "dance," a large number of English translations render as "tremble." One wonders if, in the choice of "tremble" rather than "dance," English translations have been influenced by a cultural discomfort with the body and dancing in the context of worship. This is an ecological issue as a negative view of the body is related to a more general negative view of the material world that has facilitated exploitation of Earth. In the context of a call to worship in this verse and, in the following verses, a call for all creation to rejoice and be glad, a better translation is "dance."

6. Terence E. Fretheim, *God and World in the Old Testament: A Relational Theology of Creation* (Nashville: Abingdon, 2005), 256–57.

7. Howard N. Wallace, "*Jubilate Deo omnis terra*: God and Earth in Psalm 65," in *The Earth Story in the Psalms and the Prophets*, ed. Norman Habel and Shirley Wurst, The Earth Bible, vol. 4 (Sheffield: Sheffield Academic, 2001), 57, 63.

8. Patrick D. Miller Jr., "The Poetry of Creation: Psalm 104," in *God Who Creates: Essays in Honor of W. Sibley Towner*, eds. William P. Brown and S. Dean McBride Jr. (Grand Rapids, Mich.: Eerdmans, 2000), 99; Arthur Walker-Jones, "Psalm 104: A Celebration of the *Vanua*," in *The Earth Story in the Psalms and the Prophets*, The Earth Bible, vol. 4, ed. Norman C. Habel and Shirley Wurst (Sheffield: Sheffield Academic, 2001), 93.

9. Miller, "The Poetry of Creation," 97.

10. I am indebted to Norman Habel, in a personal communication, for the insight that "Psalm 104 reverses the curse."

11. While Leviathan is not called a *nakhash* "serpent" in Ps 104:26, it is called a *nakhash* "serpent" in Isa 27:1.
12. Miller, "The Poetry of Creation," 98.
13. Ibid., 98–99.
14. Karl Löning and Zenger, *To Begin with, God Created*, trans. Omar Kaste (Collegeville, Minn.: Michael Glazier, 2000), 36.
15. Ibid.
16. The Masoretic text has "he is coming" twice, but many Hebrew manuscripts, the Syriac version, and the parallels in Ps 98:9 and 1 Chr 16:33 have only one "he is coming." The shorter reading is more probable (*Lectio brevior praeferenda est*), and the longer reading was likely the result of dittography.
17. On the choice of language in Hebrew for God's governance see p. 178 n. 18.
18. The Qere, the Cairo Geniza, and many Targums have the plural *words*. The Kethib and a number of versions have the singular *word*. Whether the word is singular or plural, it is the same Hebrew word as in verse 18, and I have italicized to emphasize the parallelism.
19. Exodus 15:25; Lev 26:46; Deut 4:1, 5, 8, 14, 45; 5:1, 31; 6:1, 20; 7:11; 11:32; 12:1; 26:16-17; Josh 24:25; 1 Sam 30:25; 1 Kg. 8:58; 9:4; 2 Kgs 17:37; 1 Chr 22:13; 2 Chr 7:17; 19:10; 33:8; Ezra 7:10; Neh 1:7; 9:13; 10:30; Pss 81:5; 147:19; Ezek 11:12; 20:18, 25; 36:27; Mal 3:22.
20. Psalms 29:3-9; 68:4, 7-10, 33-34; 93:1b-4; 97:2-5; 104:2-9, 32; 114:2-6; 135:6-7; 147:8, 16-18.
21. Psalms 104:14-15, 27-28; 111:5; 136:25; 145:15-16; 146:7; 147:9, 14.
22. Psalms 99:4; 98:9-10; 103:6; 104:35; 113:6-9; 145:14, 17; 146:7-9; 147:3, 6.
23. Psalms 68:35; 96:6, 8; 100:4; 99:9 holy mountain; 135:2 house of the LORD; 135:21 Zion / Jerusalem.
24. Frank Moore Cross, *Canaanite Myth and Hebrew Epic: Essays in the History of the Religion of Israel* (Cambridge, Mass.: Harvard University Press, 1973), 162.
25. H. L. Ginsberg, trans., "Poems about Baal and Anat," in James B. Pritchard, ed., *Ancient Near Eastern Texts Relating to the Old Testament* (3d ed.; Princeton: Princeton University Press, 1969), 140; Michael David Coogan, trans., *Stories from Ancient Canaan* (Louisville: Westminster, 1978), 112.

26. Rahab is not mentioned in the ancient Near Eastern literature that has been discovered so far, but the appearances of the name in the Hebrew Bible indicate that this is one of the primordial sea monsters that the warrior god defeats in other ancient Near Eastern versions.

27. Norman Habel and Geraldine Avent, "Rescuing Earth from a Storm God," in *The Earth Story in the Psalms and the Prophets*, The Earth Bible, vol. 4, ed. Norman Habel and Shirley Wurst (Sheffield: Sheffield Academic, 2001), 43.

28. NRSV has "of his name" in Ps 29:2a and "due his name" in 96:8a, but the Hebrew is identical.

29. Habel and Avent think the temple in verse 9 is a heavenly temple because heavenly beings were the ones called to worship at the beginning of Psalm 29 (Habel and Avent, "Rescuing Earth," 45). Even if those in the temple are people, as other commentators hold, this is still a much narrower group of worshippers than in Psalms 96 and 97.

30. Habel and Avent, "Rescuing Earth," 49.

31. Habel and Avent think that "[b]eneath the sevenfold barrage of the *qol YHWH*, the voices of Earth and Earth community are effectively silenced" (Habel and Avent, "Rescuing Earth," 47).

32. Aldo Leopold, *A Sand County Almanac: With Essays on Conservation from Round River* (New York: Oxford University Press, 1966), 158–63.

SELECTED BIBLIOGRAPHY

Adams, Carol J., ed. *Ecofeminism and the Sacred.* New York: Continuum, 1993.

Anderson, Bernhard, ed. *Creation in the Old Testament.* Philadelphia: Fortress Press, 1984.

Begrich, Joachim. "Das priesterliche Heilsorakel." *ZAW* 52 (1934): 81–92.

Braude, William G. *The Midrash on Psalms.* 2 vols. Yale Judaica Series 13. New Haven, Conn.: Yale University Press, 1954.

Brown, William P. *The Ethos of the Cosmos: The Genesis of Moral Imagination in the Bible.* Grand Rapids, Mich.: William B. Eerdmans, 1999.

_____. *Seeing the Psalms: A Theology of Metaphor.* Louisville, Ky.: Westminster John Knox, 2002.

Brown, William P. and S. Dean McBride Jr., eds. *God Who Creates: Essays in Honor of W. Sibley Towner.* Grand Rapids, Mich.: William B. Eerdmans, 2000.

Brueggemann, Walter. "Bounded by Obedience and Praise: The Psalms as Canon." *JSOT* 50 (1991): 63–92.

_____. *Israel's Praise: Doxology against Idolatry and Ideology.* Philadelphia: Fortress Press, 1988.

_____. "Response to J. Richard Middleton." *HTR* 87 (1994): 279–89.

Callender, Dexter E., Jr. *Adam in Myth and History: Ancient Israelite Perspectives on the Primal Human.* HSS 48. Winona Lake, Ind.: Eisenbrauns, 2000.

Childs, Brevard S. *Biblical Theology in Crisis.* Philadelphia: Westminster, 1970.

————. *Introduction to the Old Testament as Scripture.* Philadelphia: Fortress Press, 1979.

Clifford, Richard J. "Cosmogonies in the Ugaritic Texts and in the Bible," *Orientalia* n.s. 53 (1984): 183–201.

Coogan, Michael David, ed. *Stories from Ancient Canaan.* Louisville: Westminster, 1978.

Coupe, Laurence. *Myth.* The New Critical Idiom. Edited by John Drakakis. London: Routledge, 1997.

Cross, Frank Moore. *Canaanite Myth and Hebrew Epic: Essays in the History of the Religion of Israel.* Cambridge, Mass.: Harvard University Press, 1973.

Daly, Mary. *Beyond God the Father: Toward a Philosophy of Women's Liberation.* Boston: Beacon, 1973.

Day, John. *God's Conflict with the Dragon and the Sea.* Cambridge: Cambridge University Press, 1985.

deClaissé-Walford, Nancy L. *Introduction to the Psalms: A Song from Ancient Israel.* St. Louis: Chalice, 2004.

Dietrich, M., O. Loretz, and J. Sanmartin, eds. *The Cuneiform Alphabetic Texts from Ugarit, Ras Ibn Hani, and Other Places.* Münster: Ugarit-Verlag, 1995.

Eaton, Heather. *Introducing Ecofeminist Theologies.* Introducing Feminist Theologies 12. London: T & T Clark International, 2005.

Fretheim, Terence E. *Exodus.* Louisville, Ky.: John Knox, 1991.

————. *God and World in the Old Testament: A Relational Theology of Creation.* Nashville: Abingdon, 2005.

————. "The Plagues as Ecological Signs of Historical Disaster." *JBL* 110 (1991): 385–96.

Frye, Northrop. *Anatomy of Criticism: Four Essays.* Princeton, N.J.: Princeton University Press, 1957.

_____. *The Great Code: The Bible and Literature*. San Diego, New York, and London: Harcourt, 1982.

_____. *Words with Power: Being a Second Study of "The Bible and Literature."* New York: Viking, Penguin Books, 1990.

Gerstenberger, Erhard S. *Psalms: Part 1 with an Introduction to Cultic Poetry.* Vol. 14 of The Forms of Old Testament Literature. Edited by Rolf Knierim and Gene M. Tucker. Grand Rapids, Mich.: William B. Eerdmans, 1988.

Gray, John. *The Biblical Doctrine of the Reign of God*. Edinburgh: T. & T. Clark, 1979.

Gunkel, Hermann and Joachim Begrich. *Introduction to Psalms: The Genres of the Religious Lyric of Israel*. Translated by James D. Nogalski. Macon, Ga.: Mercer University Press, 1998. Originally published as *Einleitung in die Psalmen: die Gattungen der religiösen Lyrik Israels*. Göttinger Hankommentar zum Alten Testament. Göttingen: Vandenhoeck & Ruprecht, 1933.

Habel, Norman C. and Shirley Wurst, eds. *The Earth Story in Genesis.* Earth Bible 2. Sheffield: Sheffield Academic; Cleveland, Ohio: Pilgrim, 2000.

Habel, Norman, ed. *The Earth Story in the Psalms and the Prophets*. Earth Bible 4. Sheffield: Sheffield Academic; Cleveland: Pilgrim, 2001.

_____, ed. *Readings from the Perspective of Earth*. Earth Bible 1. Sheffield, England: Sheffield Academic; Cleveland, Ohio: Pilgrim, 2000.

Jacobsen, Thorkild. *The Treasures of Darkness: A History of Mesopotamian Religion*. New Haven, Conn.: Yale University Press, 1976.

Jameson, Fredric. "A Conversation with Fredric Jameson." *Semeia* 59 (1992): 227–237.

_____. *The Political Unconscious: Narrative as Socially Symbolic Act*. Ithaca, N.Y.: Cornell University Press, 1981.

Jeremias, Jörg. *Theophanie: Die Geschichte einer alttestamentlichen Gattung.* Wissenschaftliche Monographien zum Alten und Neuen Testament 10. 2nd ed. Neukirchen-Vluyn: Neukirchener Verlag, 1977.

Kapelrud, Arvid. "Creation in the Ras Shamra Texts." *ST* 34 (1980): 1–11.

Keck, Leander, et al., eds. *The New Interpreter's Bible*. 12 vols. Nashville: Abingdon, 1994–1998.

Keel, Othmar. *Goddesses and Trees, New Moon and Yahweh: Ancient Near Eastern Art and the Hebrew Bible*. JSOTSup 61. Sheffield: Sheffield Academic, 1998.

_____. *The Symbolism of the Biblical World: Ancient Near Eastern Iconography and the Book of Psalms*. Translated by Timothy J. Hallett. New York: Seabury, 1978.

Kerridge, Richard and Neil Sammells, eds. *Writing the Environment: Ecocriticism & Literature*. London: Zed, 1998.

Kraus, Hans-Joachim. *Psalms 1–59*. Translated by Hilton C. Oswald. Minneapolis: Fortress Press, 1993.

_____. *Psalms 60–150*. Translated by Hilton C. Oswald. Minneapolis: Fortress Press, 1993.

Lakoff, George. *Metaphors We Live By*. Chicago: University of Chicago Press, 1980.

Lawrence, Thomas B. and Nelson Phillips, "From *Moby Dick* to *Free Willy*: Macro-Cultural Discourse and Institutional Entrepreneurship in Emerging Institutional Fields," *Organization* 11 (2004): 689–711.

Leopold, Aldo. *A Sand County Almanac: With Essays on Conservation from Round River*. New York: Oxford University Press, 1966.

Levenson, Jon D. *Creation and the Persistence of Evil: The Jewish Drama of Divine Omnipotence*. Princeton, N.J.: Princeton University Press, 1994.

Lovin, Robin W. and Frank E. Reynods, eds. *Cosmology and Ethical Order: New Studies in Comparative Ethics*. Chicago: University of Chicago Press, 1985.

Macintosh, A. A. "A Consideration of Hebrew *g'r*." *VT* 19 (1969): 471–79.

Mays, James L. *The Lord Reigns: A Theological Handbook to the Psalms*. Louisville, Ky.: Westminster John Knox, 1994.

_____. "The Place of the Torah-Psalms in the Psalter." *JBL* 106 (1987): 3–12.

McCann, J. Clinton, Jr. *A Theological Introduction to the Book of Psalms: The Psalms as Torah*. Nashville: Abingdon, 1993.

McFague, Sallie. *The Body of God: An Ecological Theology.* Minneapolis: Fortress Press, 1993.

———. *Life Abundant: Rethinking Theology and Economy for a Planet in Peril.* Minneapolis: Fortress Press, 2001.

———. *Metaphorical Theology: Models of God in Religious Language.* Philadelphia: Fortress, 1982.

———. *Models of God: Theology for an Ecological, Nuclear Age.* Philadelphia: Fortress Press, 1987.

———. *Supernatural Christians: How We Should Love Nature.* Minneapolis: Fortress Press, 1997.

Middleton, J. Richard. "Is Creation Theology Inherently Conservative: A Dialogue with Walter Brueggemann." *HTR* 87 (1994): 257–77.

Miller, Patrick D., Jr. *The Divine Warrior in Early Israel.* HSM 5. Cambridge, Mass.: Harvard University Press, 1973.

———. *They Cried to the Lord: The Form and Theology of Biblical Prayer.* Minneapolis: Fortress Press, 1994.

Molin, George. "Das Motiv vom Chaoskampf im Alten Orient und in den Traditionen Jerusalems und Israels." In *Memoria Jerusalem: Freundesgabe Franz Sauer zum 70. Geburtstag,* 13–28. Graz, Austria: Akademische Druck- u. Verlagsanstalt, 1977.

Muilenburg, James. "Form Criticism and Beyond." *JBL* 88 (1969): 1–18.

Ollenburger, Ben C. "Isaiah's Creation Theology." *Ex Auditu* 3 (1987): 54–71.

Plumwood, Val. *Feminism and the Mastery of Nature.* New York: Routledge, 1993.

Primavesi, Anne. *From Apocalypse to Genesis: Ecology, Feminism and Christianity.* Minneapolis: Fortress Press, 1991.

Pritchard, James B., ed. *Ancient Near Eastern Texts Relating to the Old Testament.* 3rd ed.; Princeton, N.J.: Princeton University Press, 1969.

Reif, C. "A Note on g'r." *VT* 21 (1971): 241–44.

Saggs, H. W. F. *The Encounter with the Divine in Mesopotamia and Israel.* Jordan Lectures 1976. London: Athlone, 1978.

Scott, James C. *Domination and the Arts of Resistance: Hidden Transcripts.* New Haven, Conn.: Yale University Press, 1990.

Simkins, Ronald A. *Creator and Creation: Nature in the Worldview of Ancient Israel.* Peabody, Mass.: Hendrickson, 1994.

Wakeman, Mary K. "The Biblical Earth Monster in Cosmogonic Myth." *JBL* 88 (1969): 313–20.

_____. *God's Battle with the Monster: A Study in Biblical Imagery.* Leiden: E. J. Brill, 1973.

Walker-Jones, Arthur. "Alternative Cosmogonies in the Psalms." Ph.D. diss., Princeton Theological Seminary, 1991.

_____. "Honey from the Rock: The Contribution of God as Rock to an Ecological Hermeneutic." In *Exploring Ecological Hermeneutics*, 91–102. Edited by Norman Habel and Peter Trudinger. Symposia Series 46. Atlanta: Society of Biblical Literature, 2008.

Weems, Renita. *Battered Love: Marriage, Sex, and Violence in the Hebrew Prophets.* Overtures to Biblical Theology. Minneapolis: Fortress Press, 1995.

Westermann, Claus. *Genesis 1–11: A Commentary.* Minneapolis: Augsburg Publishing House, 1984.

_____. *Praise and Lament in the Psalms.* Translated by Keith R. Crim and Richard N. Soulen. Atlanta: John Knox, 1981.

White, Lynn, Jr. "The Historical Roots of Our Ecological Crisis." *Science* 155 (1967): 1203–7.

Wilson, Gerald Henry. *The Editing of the Hebrew Psalter.* SBLDS 76. Chico, Calif.: Scholars, 1985.

_____. "The Shape of the Book of Psalms." *Int* 46 (1992): 129–42.

_____. "Shaping the Psalter: A Consideration of Editorial Linkage in the Book of Psalms." In *Shape and Shaping of the Psalter*, 72–82. Edited by J. Clinton McCann. Sheffield: JSOT, 1993.

_____. "The Use of Untitled Psalms in the Hebrew Psalter." *ZAW* 97 (1985): 404–13.

Zimmerli, Walter. "The Place and Limit of Wisdom in the Framework of Old Testament Theology." *SJT* 17 (1964): 146–58.

INDEX OF AUTHORS AND SUBJECTS

Creator, God as, 27, 29, 84–85, 87, 88, 90, 91–108, 114, 116–119, 120–123, 124–128, 130, 131, 134, 135–143. 144, 148–151; shift in understanding of, 151–164
Cross, Frank Moore, 47, 86, 152
Cultural criticism, 13, 164

Day, John, 172n31
deClaissé-Walford, Nancy, 16, 89–90
Divine warrior, 47–52, 56, 58, 66–73, 74, 90, 152
Dualism(s), 4, 5–7, 9, 28–29, 32, 112–113, 176n36
Dualistic thinking, 5–6. *See also* binary thinking

Earth as a subject, 8–9, 137, 138, 143, 160, 163, 164, 176n40, 179n26, 179n27
Earth Bible, 7–10, 16, 133; principles, 11
Earth or Creation's voice, 8–9, 27, 107, 133, 134–138, 142–43, 150, 160, 163–4, 180n2, 182n31. *See also* Creation's praise
Ecofeminism and Ecofeminists, 5–6
Ecojustice, 5–7, 133, 144–148; principles, 8, 9, 133, 134
Ecotheology, 11
Editors and editorial activity, 15, 19–21, 32, 100
Enthronement psalms or hymns, 88, 91–93, 96, 106, 108, 116–119, 134, 144, 150, 151, 156, 157
Enuma Elish, 47, 82, 92
Ethos, 13, 16, 32, 86

Five books of the Psalter, 15, 21, 163
Free Willy, 73, 75–79
Fretheim, Terence E., 85, 86, 97, 98, 108, 114, 137, 177n13
Frye, Northrop, 11–13, 73, 166n24

Genre, 12–17, 21, 24, 27, 32, 37–42, 44, 45, 51, 54, 57, 58–60, 62, 63, 64, 66, 67, 72, 79, 81, 86–90 *passim*, 100, 102, 105–6, 108, 148, 154, 164, 167n25, 170n4, 173n1, 179n23
Genre criticism, 14–15, 58–6
Genre critics, 37, 42, 57,
Gerstenberger, Erhard S. 20, 102, 170n4, 173n1
Gore, Al, 2
Gray, John, 82
Greenberg, Moshe, 170n11
Greenpeace, 77
Gunkel, Hermann, 20, 170n4, 173n1

Habel, Norman, 30, 133, 157, 159,176n36, 182n29, 182n31
Hallel psalms, 101
Hallelujah psalms, 99, 100, 101, 102, 103, 130
Hallelujah, 95, 99, 100; translation of, 101
Historical criticism, 9, 10, 11, 14
Human rights, 111–112

Image of God, 4, 7, 10, 11, 54, 63, 69, 70, 71, 86, 88, 98, 114, 118, 135, 139, 145, 151–154, 160, 163
Imagery, 2, 11, 13, 16, 29, 36, 42, 49–52, 54–56, 58, 60, 62–63, 65, 66–73, 78–80, 84–86, 100, 101, 103–109 *passim*, 116–119 *passim*, 129, 135, 137, 138, 145, 148–151, 155, 156, 160; typical or recurring, 42, 44, 56, 60, 66, 79, 86, 87, 90, 92, 95, 96, 148, 149
Images, 6, 12, 13, 14, 16, 24, 29, 36, 43–45, 47, 49, 50–52, 53, 55, 56, 86, 96, 108, 109, 142, 148, 160, 164; typical or recurring, 36, 86, 148
Interconnectedness, 9, 31; principle of, 8, 9, 134

Interdependence, 6, 7, 9, 29, 63, 111, 140

Interrelationship, 6–7, 29, 63, 65, 111, 133, 134, 140, 142

Intrinsic value or worth, 4, 32, 36, 49, 133–34, 137, 139–40, 142–43; principle of, 8, 9

Jameson, Fredric, 11, 12, 126
Joüon, P. 173n8

Kapelrud, Arvid, 82
Kee, James M., 166n21

Lawrence, Thomas B., 76
Levenson, Jon D., 178n22.
Leviathan, 47, 66, 67, 73–75, 78, 79, 121–22, 123, 140, 141, 155, 171n25, 178n22, 180n11
Liberation. *See* Creation: and liberation or justice
Lion King, 35–36, 56
Lion(s), 30, 37, 45, 56, 61, 139, 140, 141, 142, 171 n 24
Löning, Karl, 119, 141
Lord of the Rings, 53, 55–56
Lotan, 47
Lovin, Robin W., 85

Macintosh, A. A., 173n8
Mays, James L., 20
McCann, J. Clinton, 20, 130
McCarthy, Dennis, 82
McFague, Sallie, 10
Middleton, Richard, 16, 113, 114
Midrash Tehillim, 21
Miller, Patrick D., Jr., 94, 97, 141, 170n11
Moby Dick, 73–80
Myth criticism, 11–12
Myth, 11, 12, 47, 73, 82, 83, 85, 92, 114, 117, 149, 152; Ugaritic, 47, 50, 135, 179n2. *See also* Divine warrior

Mythic language and allusions, 69, 73, 79, 107, 155
Mythic pattern, 36, 42, 47, 48, 53, 56, 67, 68, 69, 72, 73, 74, 78, 82, 84, 92, 96, 152, 155, 171n25
Mythos, 12–13, 47, 60, 66, 86

Narrative, 10, 13, 29, 30, 47, 48, 49, 52, 55, 56, 60, 96, 110, 164; implied, 22, 24, 36, 42–44, 48, 54, 56, 60, 80, 86, 87, 115, 148–151; pattern or structure, 12–16, 17, 48–49, 52, 53, 54, 56, 58, 63–73, 78, 79, 96, 100, 107, 116, 119; typical, 32, 58
New Orleans, 1, 6, 111

Ollenburger, Ben, 83

Phillips, Nelson, 76
Pit, 38, 41, 42, 48, 51, 53, 56, 79, 96, 172n34. *See also* Sheol

Refuge, 19, 29, 37, 38, 39, 42, 46, 55, 56
Reif, S. C., 173n8
Reinhartz, Adele, 166n21
Reynolds, Frank E., 85
Richards, Kent Harold, 174n10
Royal psalms, 19–20, 154
Royal theology, 112, 114–17, 119, 122, 154–55

Scharbert, Josef, 174n10
Scott, James C., 121
Shape of the Psalter. *See* Canonical shape
Sheol, 23, 42, 48, 51, 79. *See also* Pit
Siha, Sandra, 32
Simkins, Ronald A., 86
Songs of Ascent, 99, 100, 101, 102, 156
Storm Theophany, 67–68, 70, 82, 84–85, 86, 87, 96, 98, 101, 102,

INDEX OF SCRIPTURE CITATIONS

	28:4a	41			35:20	38
	28:6	40			35:22b-24a	40
	28:7-8	39			35:26	42
	28:9	39			35:28	40
Psalm	29	88, 157–60		Psalm	36	19, 44
	29:1	158			36:2	22
	29:1b-2	158			36:3	22
	29:3	27			36:6	32
	29:3-9	106		Psalm	37	19, 44
	29:8-9	158			37:1	23
	29:9	27, 158			37:2	31
Psalm	31:1	37			37:5	23
	31:1-2	40			37:7	23
	31:2, 3	54			37:11	23
	31:3b-4a	40, 42			37:12	22
	31:7-8	40			37:14	23
	31:9a	40			37:19	23
	31:9-11	38			37:20	25
	31:13	38			37:22	23
	31:14-15	39			37:29	23
	31:15b-17a	40			37:30	22
	31:17	51			37:32	23
	31:17b-18	42			37:34	23
	31:19-20, 23	39			37:35	31
	31:21-22	41			37:40	23
Psalm	32:6	27		Psalm	40:2	51
Psalm	33	20, 88, 115–116		Psalm	41:31	21
	33:4-7	115		Psalm	42:9	54
	33:4-9	149		Psalm	43:3	49
	33:6	106, 153		Psalm	44	66, 71
	33:7	27, 153			44:4-5	58
	33:10	115, 153			44:8	59
	33:15	106, 149			44:9-16	58, 65
	33:16-17	115			44:11	62
Psalm	34:10	45			44:17	59
Psalm	35:1	37			44:19	58, 65
	35:4-6	42			44:22	58
	35:7	38			44:23	59
	35:8	42			44:24-25	58
	35:11-12	38			44:26	59, 64
	35:15-16	38		Psalm	46:1-7	47
	35:17	17, 45			46:3	27
	35:18	40		Psalm	47	88, 106

	104:26	140, 141		106:22	95
	104:27	141		106:35	94
	104:27-28	113		106:39	94
	104:27-30	120		106:47	69
	104:28	93, 94, 141		106:47b	60
	104:29	142		106:48	21
	104:29-30	139, 142, 149	Psalm	107	99, 100
	104:30	84, 141		107:4-8	100
	104:31	94, 141		107:10-16	100
	104:31-32	47		107:17-22	100
	104:32	142		107:23-32	100
	104:33-34	94		107:33	27
	104:35	122, 139		107:33-38, 41	100
Psalm	105	20, 94–97, 107		107:39-41	100
	105:2	94, 95	Psalm	108	66, 71
	105:2-3	94		108:7	71
	105:5	94, 95		108:7-10	61
	105:7	95		108:9	71
	105:16	97		108:11	71
	105:24	97		108:13	71
	105:28	97	Psalm	111	20
	105:29	97		111:5	108
	105:30	97	Psalm	112	19, 20
	105:31	97		112:1	22
	105:32-33	98		112:2	23
	105:33	27		112:4	22
	105:34-35	98		112:5	22, 23
	105:36	98		112:9	21, 22, 23
	105:39	98	Psalm	114	101–102, 103, 107
	105:40-41	98		114:3-7	47
	105:41	28		114:8	28
Psalm	106	66, 68, 69, 71,	Psalm	115	101-102
		95–99, 107		115:15	85, 88, 102
	106:7	94–95, 98	Psalm	119	19, 20, 23,
	106:8-12	68			100–101
	106:9	68, 69, 98		119:6	23
	106:11	27, 98		119:23	23
	106:13	94, 98		119:42	23
	106:11	98		119:51	23
	106:15	98		119:69	23
	106:17	98		119:72	23
	106:17-18	69		119:73	101
	106:18	98, 98		119:86-7	23